Praise for *Meadow Skipper:* The Untold Story

Roget's Thesaurus provides us with alternate meanings of emphasis to words throughout our vast language. In this case, however, *Roget's Thesaurus* provides us with little in describing this work of written art by authors Victoria Howard and Bob Marks. Quite simply, *Meadow Skipper: The Untold Story* is a treasure.

For those of us who have enjoyed the brilliant and unparalleled history of the Standardbred during Skipper's lifetime, this book recaptures those great memories for you from the moment a new arrival, subsequently named Meadow Skipper, took his first breath, throughout a lifetime and beyond as the legacy of this great horse gets even greater, seemingly with every race contested to this very day.

For those of you who were "foaled" in an era where you, quite sadly, missed out on some of Meadow Skipper's greatest performances on the racetrack, the authors take you, almost by hand, everywhere—in the foaling shed, on the racetrack, in the sulky, in the announcer's booth, and, finally, what can only be described as witnessing a reincarnation through sons, daughters, grandsons, granddaughters, and beyond. Indeed, this is a scripture for everyone and should not be missed.

You will be able to "hear" the Meadow Skipper hoof prints thundering over the track as he stretches his potential with every stride during his grand racing career. And, too, you'll hear the hoof prints of his prodigy as they too perform and inevitably, change the very history of Standardbred racing.

Yes, the untold story is untold no more.

—John Berry
Communicators Hall of Fame

"Not only did Meadow Skipper have a profound influence on the Standardbred racing and breeding world; the indelible mark that he left on the hearts of his fans rivaled that of the great Secretariat. Visitors flocked to see him and some went as far as to take a lock of his mane as a lasting memento. Told from Meadow Skipper's perspective, this entertaining story immediately engages those familiar with his accomplishments as well as someone who's meeting him for the first time."

—Lynne Myers

"This is not just a splendid book, it is a spectacular one. It can only be described as a labor of love, a fastidiously researched and profusely illustrated account of the history of harness racing's greatest stallion—Meadow Skipper. Superbly written and highly recommended. A real- life fairy tale."

—Allan Jay Friedman
Composer, lyricist, author, and Emmy Award winner

"Meadow Skipper's influence on the Standardbred breed is well-known. What's not as apparent is how that came to be. In *Meadow Skipper: the Untold Story*, the authors, in a meticulous yet wholly entertaining way, leave no stone unturned. From the serendipity of his conception, to the tantalizingly told on-track battles, to where we are today, the book is a page-turner for anyone who loves the sport of harness racing, or racing in general."

—Dean Towers

"It is fitting that the contributions of Meadow Skipper to harness racing and the Standardbred horse breed are now documented in a book. As one of only two horses in Kentucky's Bluegrass horse country to be embalmed and buried, Meadow Skipper was a legend whose story comes to life in this unique book by Victoria Howard and Bob Marks."

—Kathy Parker

"In 2013 when Captain Treacherous was going for the Cane up at Tioga, my mind flashed back fifty years almost to the day when I saw Meadow Skipper beating Overtrick in the Cane at Yonkers back in 1963. Little did I know back then that Bob Marks and Victoria Howard would someday write a book entitled *Meadow Skipper: The Untold Story* and I'd be able to relive some of the greatest racing moments in my harness racing years. This book is an absolute treasure and I've already ordered twenty-five copies to pass out to my friends come Holiday time. Great work, you two!"

—Myron Bell

"Meadow Skipper's story is one of harness racing's great tales of serendipity and triumph that was instrumental in irrevocably changing the Standardbred breed. Bob Marks and Victoria Howard warmly detail how incredibly close the breed was to missing out on its most influential sire."

—Dave Briggs

"I've yet to read it, but those that have tell me that *Meadow Skipper: The Untold Story* is great and moving and unlike any other horse book ever written."

—Murray Brown

10/6/15

MEADOW
SKIPPER

Enjoy!

Victoria M Howard

MEADOW SKIPPER

"The Untold Story"

An unofficial autobiography
as told to
VICTORIA M. HOWARD
and BOB MARKS

TATE PUBLISHING
AND **ENTERPRISES**, LLC

Published by Tate Publishing & Enterprises, LLC
127 E. Trade Center Terrace | Mustang, Oklahoma 73064 USA
1.888.361.9473 | www.tatepublishing.com

Tate Publishing is committed to excellence in the publishing industry. The company reflects the philosophy established by the founders, based on Psalm 68:11,
"The Lord gave the word and great was the company of those who published it."

Book design copyright © 2015 by Tate Publishing, LLC. All rights reserved.
Cover design by Maria Louella Mancao
Interior design by Jomar Ouano

Published in the United States of America

ISBN: 978-1-68187-954-3
Pets / Horses
15.07.28

Meadow Skipper

I would like to dedicate this book to three men: first, to Joe Lighthill for having the insight to totally whip my ass at Hollywood Park. This probably saved the harness industry and myself from total disaster. Second, to Mr. Norman Woolworth for having the guts to take a chance on buying me and giving me a great life. And third, to Mr. Earle Avery for steering me to those insanely rough, parked out miles so I could demonstrate that I just might be the Rocky Balboa of standardbreds.

—Meadow Skipper

Acknowledgements

We would like to thank all the people who have contributed in helping to write this book. The pictures, the information, and articles that were given are greatly appreciated.

Our gratitude goes to the following:

Mr. Dean Hoffman, whose extensive writings on Meadow Skipper and the Hal Dale line in general provided such superb reference.

Ms. Janet Terhune and the entire staff at the Hall of Fame of the Trotter, for providing the photos and historical references from the journals on file there.

Ms. Kathy Parker, for providing vivid memories of Meadow Skipper's funeral from the *Horseman and Fair World* magazine in addition to those memories extracted from the column of Maryjean Wall, racing writer from the *Lexington Herald-Leader*.

Ms. Kendra Casselman, for her unpublished manuscript about Meadow Skipper that provided invaluable reference and statistical material.

Mr. Eric Cherry and the staff of Champion Communications, for graciously providing the South Florida office in which so much of *The Untold Story* got cowritten and coedited.

Mr. John Berry, who has supplied us with pictures of Meadow Skipper and has been a tremendous help to us while writing the book.

Our special thanks also go to Joe Fitzgerald, Don Daniels, Tom Grossman, Tom Charters, Myron Bell, Murray Brown, Roger Huston, Harvey Robbins, Katya Airas and Lawrence Cohen for providing the anecdotes, pictures, and statistics used in this book.

And we want to especially thank Mr. Meadow Skipper for graciously consenting to tell his story as it actually happened.

Finally, we want to give our special thanks to our sponsors: Steve and Cindy Stewart of Hunterton Farms at Stoner Creek.

Contents

PART II: BECOMING A SIRE AND HIS AMAZING OFFSPRING

Authors' Thoughts

As long as I can remember from my old handicapping and betting days, I always approached the horse with a degree of skepticism in terms of "make me like you." Do something. Call me on the phone. Tell me how much heart you have. Generally speaking, once you've got me, I'll probably be yours forever.

I first became aware of Meadow Skipper in one of those classic Mary Louise MacGregor training columns from Orlando's Ben White Raceway featured in the *Harness Horse* magazine each week.

The tall Meadow Skipper colt was cheerful clocking his training mile in 2:30 according to Mary Louis MacGregor. Mary Louise would time each horse's individual workout and would often include a comment as to how the horse looked doing it.

At that point, I knew Countess Vivian as the dam of Countess Adios, the great filly who beat the boys in two of the three Triple Crown legs that year. She was a gutsy filly with brilliant speed that obviously was not afraid of taking on the "big boys"!

From the time I learned to read a program, I was always fascinated by the breeding part and was initially convinced that there were but two kinds of harness horses—Hanovers or Adioses.

The Hanovers could be a variety of sires like Star's Pride, Hoot Mon, Knight Dream, Tar Heel, or even Adios. But all those Adios horses, like Adios Butler, Adios Harry, and Adios Boy, were all sired by one horse: Adios!

I remember that this tall colt named Meadow Skipper equaled or set the season's record for two-year-old pacers out of Hollywood Park, but I had no idea how good he might be in that it was not a major stakes race.

Fast forward six months to the Commodore at Roosevelt Raceway in June of 1963 when I finally got a look at this Meadow Skipper as he erupted from the clouds to be up in time, winning an elimination of the Commodore and beating Country Don, Marston Hanover, Timely Beauty, and Steady Beau. Meadow Skipper was now big-time!

Meadow Skipper wound up getting sold in midsummer to Norman Woolworth for a rumored $150,000 principally because "well, he can't beat the great Overtrick."

Apparently, Mr. Woolworth's trainer/driver Earle Avery, a rather crusty septuagenarian, had other ideas, and as you will discover, Skipper did indeed beat Overtrick fair and square, although I wasn't sure at the time. Back then there were no replays, and you generally only saw the race one time. Therefore, it wasn't until I had watched a thirty-minute documentary on New York television entitled *A Colt Named Overtrick*, in which the incredible fighting heart of Meadow Skipper was so prominently displayed, that I became a true Meadow Skipper fan.

Victoria, my coauthor and I, are both advocates in the harness racing business and have both been involved in one aspect or another for over forty years each. It is sad to say that Standardbred racing has always seemed to fall second to Thoroughbred racing. There have been many successful books and movies on Thoroughbreds such as Secretariat, Northern Dancer and Seabiscuit, but other than *Crazy Good: The True Story of Dan Patch, the Most Famous Horse in America* and *Big Bum: The Story of Bret Hanover*, there have been few that made the best seller list or became a movie based on the life of a champion harness stallion.

When Victoria, who had just finished co- writing and published the book *Roosevelt Raceway: Where It All Began*, approached me to cowrite a book on perhaps a unique harness horse, Meadow Skipper, I didn't hesitate a minute.

Meadow Skipper's story is an incredible one, and in so many ways, he was the equine equivalent to the cinema's Rocky Balboa. It is our wish that through him, we can reap some feel-good publicity for the harness industry by spotlighting a true underdog who became a legend in his own time.

—Bob Marks

———◆———

Ever since I was a child, I've yearned to be around horses. To me, they are by far the most spectacular animals ever created by God. As strong and as big as they may appear, they are really fragile and gentle animals.

When I was a senior in high school, my stepfather took me to a harness racing track near where we lived. From the moment I laid eyes on those huge but delicate creatures gliding around the track pulling a race bike, it was love at first sight. Like an addict who feels they cannot live without a certain drug, I was hooked. I didn't want to go to college or continue my modeling career. All I wanted was to work with horses.

My boyfriend and I claimed a mare at Wheeling Downs for $2,500 called Who Du Girl. We self-taught ourselves how to train along with the help we got from other trainers and veterinarians (especially Doc Parry), who were only too happy to teach a couple of young ambitious kids the ins and outs of the business.

Luckily (or maybe not so luckily), Who Du Girl won her very first race, knocking four seconds off her lifetime mark. With that win and the high it gave me, it hooked me for life. I thought, *Wow, this is easy!*

Throughout the next forty years, I trained, bred, raced, and owned hundreds of standardbreds. I've loved every one of them and always will.

When I became a writer, I chose relationships as my genre. Although I loved to write, my heart remained with the horses. After relocating to South Florida, I took the plunge and bought a couple of Florida-bred horses to race at Pompano. I would occasionally go to the barn and help my trainer with the grooming. Once again, I was caught hook, line, and sinker! I decided to combine my two passions together: writing about what I feel is the most wonderful career that anyone can have: harness racing.

After cowriting a book about Roosevelt Raceway, the racetrack that actually launched nighttime harness racing, I asked my friend, author, and Hall of Famer Bob Marks to collaborate with me and write a book about the most unlikely horse who became the greatest sire in the history of harness racing: Meadow Skipper.

It's strange how life takes you down certain paths. I feel so blessed to be writing a book about the super stallion that was foaled near my home racetrack, The Meadows, and about some of the people who have positively influenced me in the sport of harness racing. I was one of the lucky ones who got their start in the business at the Washington, Pennsylvania racetrack, along with several young men who would go on to become some of the best harness drivers and trainers in the industry.

Dave "Palone Ranger" Palone, David "Purple Jesus" Miller, and Brian "The White Knight" Sears were just a few of the young men who had dreams of stardom and of making a name in the business. Friends of mine, Ron and Mickey Burke, also started at The Meadows and today are the most successful team in the industry. Roger "The Voice" Huston, who is my dear friend, is undoubtedly one of the best, if not *the best*, racing announcer in the history of harness racing. Roy Davis, with his fantastic stable and driver/trainer Dick Stillings, popped out world records from the likes of Jaguar Spur, Barberry Spur, and all the other Spurs who trained from this home base. And of course, the Ambassador himself, Delvin Miller, the owner of the Meadowlands Farm and the trainer of so many superstars.

This book was written to help enlighten people on our incredible sport—standardbred racing—and hopefully put it back on the map where it rightfully belongs. And last but not least, it was written to introduce the greatest sire since Adam, the Rocky Balboa of standardbreds—the incomparable Meadow Skipper.

—Victoria M Howard

Foreword

Meadow Skipper: The Untold Story is part fiction and part nonfiction. It is a book that is composed from facts and information known to be accurate. The authors are not liable for anything that may be found to be untrue. This is a unique book for the story is told by the main character himself, Meadow Skipper, as he narrates it to the authors.

This is a delightful, animated tale written for people of all ages and from all walks of life. We are about to take you on an incredible journey into the life and times of the most unlikely horse to recreate an entire breed in his own image—Meadow Skipper.

> *This is the story of my life. I was the underdog who many thought of as "just another Dale Frost colt." I beat the odds by being sired out of convenience rather than by choice. Then, by the grace of God, I remained entire when they wanted to castrate me. Even then, they didn't believe in me as I got sold to new owners because my old owners thought I couldn't beat the superhorse, Overtrick.*
>
> *In my life I've been called many things: the Rocky Balboa of standardbreds, the greatest sire since Adam, and a sulking, stubborn SOB, but my fans and friends*

just call me Skip. I hope you enjoy my story, for yes, I was a little obstinate and hard to handle at times, but through it all, I really did do it my way!

The Family Tree of Meadow Skipper

The Abbe p, 2:04

Abbedale p,2:01.4   Daisydale D

Hal Dale   Margaret Hal   Argot Hal 2:07.1

b p,6,2:02.1 m $595   b p, 2, 2:19 .1

Margaret Polk

Dale Frost   Raider p, 1:59   Peter Volo 4, 2:02

blk p, 1:58 m $204, 117   Nelda Dillon

Galloway   Bethel   David Guy p3, 2:05

b p, 2:04.4 h $5,294

Meadow Skipper   Annotation p,2:2:18

br p,3, 1:55.1m $428,057   Kings Counsel   Volomite   Peter Volo

b p, 6, 1:58.1 $44,930   br 3, 2:03.1 $32,649   br. 4, 2:02m $44

Cita Frisco

Margaret Spangler   Guy Axworthy

b. p, 2:02.1   4, T:208.3

Maggie Winderp, 3, 2:06

Napolean Direct p,1:59.3

Gay Forbes p,5, 2:18

Countess Vivian   Billy Direct

b p, 3, 1:59 m $43,262   b p, 4, T 1:55 m $12,040

Fillys Direct p,3,2:06

Calumet Edna p,2,2:19   Peter the Brewer 4, 2:02.1

Broncho Queen p,2, 2:09

Meadow Skipper

PART I

The Start of a Legacy

1

How It All Began

"A racehorse is an animal that can take several thousand people for a ride at the same time."

Hal Dale, grandsire of Meadow Skipper

The early 1900s
Ohio

I was told this is how my legacy really began. I will start the story with my matriarch grandmother. Her name was The Broncho.

The tale begins in 1898 when a mare was born named The Broncho. The Broncho was a typical standardbred of that vintage for she was slow to develop and struggled through many five-heat races as part of the education process. Interestingly, The Broncho finally got it together in 1906 at the age of eight when she competed in America's Midwest against a mare named Citation (p, 2:01.1). Ironically, The Broncho was the fourth dam of Countess Vivian, dam of Meadow Skipper.

> *My great-grandma was what many horseman call "a crazy, hot mare," for she was prone to throw tantrums and destroyed many sulkies if she didn't get her way. I'm sure that's why they named her The Broncho.*

In 1906, The Broncho was sent against the fence at Galesburg, Illinois, and paced in at 2:00.3/4, a half second off the world record for mares. After that win, The Broncho was sent off to the breeding ranks where she would leave but three foals with records. One of whom was named Broncho Queen who eventually passed into ownership of Lexington's Calumet Farm, back in the days when that farm was as prominent in standardbred circles as it was later to become in thoroughbred racing.

After being bred to Peter the Brewer in 1930, Broncho Queen produced a filly named Calumet Edna, who was later sold to Pennsylvania interests for the substantial sum of $585. (At this time, the Depression had plummeted America's economy; thus, the price tag was considered high.) Calumet Edna paced to a 2:08.1 mark and was sold in 1940 for $150. It was during this time that the fastest harness horse in the world, a horse named Billy Direct (4, T 1:55), was standing stud for the first time in Northern Ohio.

A local horseman named William Murray decided to buy a few mares to breed to the Champion—one being Calumet Edna. Shy of one year later, Edna had her Billy Direct foal that was named Filly Direct. As a yearling, Filly Direct was sold to a restaurateur from Ohio named Christy Hayes, a very big influence in my life, for five hundred dollars. Filly Direct had the misfortune of racing while war was raging in Europe, so the opportunities for her were limited; but the mare proved herself by beating off the colts at the Ohio fairs.

At the same time they purchased Filly Direct, Hayes's wife, Vivian, gave birth to their only child, a son. To Christy Hayes, the mare was not just a horse; she was a daughter to him. In fact, the proud yet nervous owner would get so riled up before the mare raced that the doctor had to administer a calming pill to him before the races.

Filly Direct showed great ability as a two-year-old, battling and often beating the colts at the Ohio fairs. She was a great racehorse who won the Horseman Futurity Pace at three. Thereafter, in the Little Brown Jug preview at Delaware, Filly Direct finished 2—3 in the pair of heats behind noted Scotland pacer, Eddie Havens. Later that year, the mare took a mark of 2:06.3 on a half-mile track but never reduced it. This is a prime example of a racehorse with a misleading record, as she/he was often on the wire in races much faster than the mark they carried to their grave.

In 1949, Filly Direct had her first foal by the big Volomite pacer, King's Counsel. The foal was named Country Christy after her owner, Christy Hayes. The next year Christy had another filly that they named Countess Vivian after Christy's wife.

Countess Vivian, by the way is my mom.

Al Winger broke Countess Vivian in Florida at Orlando's Ben White training center and eventually sent her on the time-honored trail of Grand Circuit in 1952. She won a heat at the Goshen Mile track but lost the race off to Frances Jewell. A race-off happens when individual heat winners return for an extra and deciding heat against each other. That winner then becomes the race winner.

Due to an unexpected circumstance, Filly Direct was sold to Poplar Hill Farms in Lexington, but fortunately, the Hayes family retained her 1950 yearling filly called Countess Vivian. Countess Vivian grew up to be a gorgeous majestic mare. She was one tough racehorse. She won a heat at Goshen and set a season's mark in 2:06.2, while Precious Hal grabbed the other heat in the identical time. In the race-off, Vivian would enter the record books as the champion for juvenile fillies for three heats divided. She paced her final quarter in a sizzling 29.2. Later in the fall that year, Vivian time trialed at Lexington, with fractions of 31, 1:01.2, 1:31.2 and out in 2:03.

By this time, many took notice of the new "princess of pacing fillies." The big filly was so easy to handle that her owner, Hayes, took pride in training her himself at the Ohio State Fairgrounds. He compared the mare to a big Cadillac that had a perfect stroke and seven gears.

Vivian was not only considered a member of the Hayes family but was the only horse Christy trained and practically lived with. Extremely confident in his mare's ability, Hayes entered her in the Little Brown Jug against the colts, where she left from post-position seven, gained cover, and, in a thrilling stretch drive, missed by a bare nose at the wire. In heat two, Countess Vivian was parked the entire mile and finished ninth. In the final heat of the Jug, the mare raced her heart out, finishing fastest of all, but wound up a more-than-respectable third against the boys.

A parked-out trip, eh? Why does that sound familiar?

The race that so many remember was when Countess Vivian beat fifteen other fillies in a stake at Good Time Park in Goshen with the Midas of Meadow Lands himself, Mr. Del Miller, in the sulky. She timed in at 2:00.3/5 and was back in 2:00 .1. Those who watched her said she went on two ferocious trips and was really oozing class.

That year, Vivian started twenty-nine times, ending with thirteen wins and earnings of $28,717. This was quite impressive for a filly, especially one who tried colts on more than one occasion. Although she raced well the following year, she was not up to her previous form. She won but two races: the final triumph coming in 2:05 at Sportsman's Park in a $2,500 race for fillies and mares. Countess Vivian was then retired and sent to Del Miller's Meadow Lands Farm, specifically to be bred to Adios.

For the next four years, the consummated union between Vivian and Adios resulted in four fillies: Adios Vivian, Countess Adios, Vivian's Adios, and Skipper's Countess. Countess Adios was by far the best of the bunch.

You're going to be hearing a lot about Countess Adios, who happens to be my half sister, in this book.

In fact, Miller himself once said, "She was perhaps the greatest pacing mare I ever trained."

In 1959, Vivian would change bed partners when Adios unexpectedly foundered. Miller asked the farm manager,

Harry Harvey, to call Mr. Hayes and inform him of the need to breed his mare to another stallion—in this case, the other farm stallion, Dale Frost.

At first, Hayes said he would prefer to wait for Adios's recovery, but Miller told him he wasn't sure if this would happen during that breeding season. Although Hayes wasn't convinced, Miller persisted until he gave in. Miller intentionally refused to take any phone calls in case Mr. Hayes was having a change of heart. Countess Vivian was bred that same day and got in foal.

Unfortunately, Hayes died later that year never knowing that he had bred a horse whose prepotency would dominate pacing pedigrees for the final three decades of the twentieth century and into the first two decades of the twenty-first century. After the death of Hayes, Countess Vivian, back in foal to Adios and along with her Dale Frost weanling, was sold to Hugh A. Grant.

Besides Meadow Skipper, Vivian was the dam of Countess Adios (1:57.3) and Tarport Count (1:59.3). The latter of the two was fast enough but was known to be fractious and would break stride on occasion; thus, he never fulfilled his genetic potential.

Meanwhile, Countess Adios was a great filly pacer, and to this day is considered amongst the best fillies that ever lived. No other filly in history has ever approached her record of two Triple Crown triumphs against the colts.

Yep, my sister sure was a good one, but that only put pressure on me for she was a tough act to follow.

Countess Vivian's sire was King Counsel by the legendary trotting sire Volomite, who was known to also get his fair share of good pacers. Back in those days it was not uncommon for many standardbred stallions to be double-gaited sires—producing both trotters and pacers. Volomite, through sons like Kings Counsel, Sampson Hanover, and Poplar Byrd, was in the process of establishing a pacing line.

Coincidentally, that line still survives today through Sampson Hanover's son Sampson Direct. Sampson Direct is the sire of Direct Scooter, who is responsible for Matt Scooter, the sire of present-day stallion Mach Three. The line extends from Mach Three through his superstar son Somebeachsomewhere, and that one's leading son Captain Treacherous.

Whew, that's a mouthful!

Although there was trotting blood from Vivian's immediate male line, her dam Filly Direct was by pacing stalwart Billy Direct. Countess Vivian was a fluid pacer, as was her great daughter Countess Adios, who raced free-legged without the hobbles, similar to her maternal great-grandsire, Billy Direct. Unfortunately, Vivian's first colt didn't take after his dam and sister for he was more awkward-going and had a long sweeping gait reminiscent of his smallish sire, Dale Frost. As it would be, Meadow Skipper inherited his robust size from his dam, not his smallish sire or grandsire.

It was the summer of 1927 when Indian horse breeder Abe McClamrock had nine yearling colts turned out at Clinton Country fairgrounds at Frankfort. McClamrok had made arrangements with local veterinarian Dr. Erdle to castrate all the colts. One by one, the unsuspecting yearlings were led out to have their manhood taken away.

When the ninth and final colt was led out, the veterinarian refused to castrate him saying, "He was too fine a colt, and if they wanted him gelded they would have to find another vet to do the job."

Lucky colt number 9 was returned to his stall and remained entire.

---◆---

In life, we believe that there are no coincidences and that things happen for a reason. That colt was not supposed to be gelded that day, or any day thereafter, for there was something very important that he would have to do.

> *It's lucky for me and the world of harness racing that Dr. Erdle knew something good when he saw it. Thanks, Doc. The entire harness industry owes you an eternal debt of gratitude.*

Colt Number 9 was named Hal Dale (Abbedale—Margaret Hal), who became a foundation pacing stallion, siring great sires Adios and Good Time, besides Irish Hal, Keystoner, Walter McKlyo, and Russet Hal. He also sired Meadow Skipper's sire, Dale Frost.

> *Hey, that's my pop!*

The second dam of Dale Frost was named Bethel (p, 2:03), and his first dam named Galloway had a record of 2:04 1/5. In 1948, Galloway became the property of Roy Amos of Edinburg, Indiana. The first time he bred her he went to the tall, well-respected Volomite pacer, King's Counsel. That resulted in a filly named Jackie Frost (p, 2, T2:07). The next year, Amos shipped her to Indiana's pride and joy, Hal Dale. The result of this encounter was a small but handsome colt they christened Dale Frost.

Guess I got some of my looks from him and my size from my mother.

————◆————

Hal Dale's offspring dominated and extended pacing pedigrees and, through son Adios and particularly through grandson Meadow Skipper, appears multiple times in the extended family tree of just about *every* pacing horse alive today. Hal Dale couldn't actually race until age six, owing to severe tendon problems, a trait that his grandson Meadow Skipper would inherit. In all, Hal Dale started nine times with eight wins, taking a mark of 2:02.1/4.

Breeder Leo McNamara of Two Gaits Farm took a liking to a son of Hal Dale named Frisco Dale and offered to purchase the stallion. Trainer Sep Palin originally nixed the idea, claiming Hal Dale was much too small. But after Frisco Dale finished a sharp second in the Fox State, Palin changed his mind, and McNamara purchased the stallion for two thousand dollars. In the first year of breeding, Hal Dale's service fee was all of fifty dollars.

————◆————

Don Millar, the esteemed USTA Vice President, recalled Hal Dale as one who stamped his foals looks and conformation wise. When a stallion's offspring tend to look like him, it is called "stamping". At the 1952 Tattersalls sale, Del Miller liked the Hal Dale colt named Dale Frost but got outbid by Billy Haughton, who bought him for $3,100.

Breeder Roy Amos was not satisfied with the price, insisting the colt was undersold. He then inquired if Haughton would take a quick profit and resell. Amos gave Haughton an extra one thousand dollars, big money in those days, and took him back. Soon after, he resold him to Charles Provost of Pittsburgh for a hefty ten thousand dollars.

So in a matter of a few months, this "little horse" had his registration papers changed four different times. He was originally owned by Amos, then Haughton, then back to Amos, and finally to Provost, who owned him until his death.

———◆———

Dale Frost, like Hal Dale, was a small but sturdy colt that quickly proved to be one of the leaders of his freshman crop. But according to Miller, he had one small problem: he was so damn small that he'd try to duck under the starting gate.

Dale Frost started his stakes career by winning the Meadowlands Farm Pace in straight heats of 2:00.1 and 2:02. Several horsemen clocked the colt in 2:00 flat, but the visuamatic timer's 2:00 1/5 stood.

In the Geers Stake at Goshen, Dale Frost won identical heats in 2:01.3, matching the standard held by Little Brown Jug winner and sire Knight Dream. In addition, the great Tar Heel's single dash standard of 2:03 also fell by the wayside.

"Dale Frost had a long, sweeping gait for a little horse," Miller once said. "He was kind of a daisy cutter who couldn't leave the gate very fast." This was another trait that would later haunt his most famous son, Meadow Skipper.

See, my gate problems were inherited, not invented.

———— ◆ ————

At two and three, Dale Frost made sixty-two starts, but he soon developed a weak front ankle that would hamper him throughout his aged career. At four years old, he headed to the post only twelve times. At ages five and six, he raced and infrequently conquered the likes of Bachelor Hanover, Duane Hanover, Diamond Hal, Keystoner, and even his old nemesis, Adios Harry.

On August 23, 1956, as Vernon New York experienced one of its worst windstorms, Duane Hanover churned the fractions of 26 4/5, 57 1/5, and 1:28, while Dale Frost swept from behind to win in 1:58 3/5. At age six, the now tireless little warrior made forty starts. He won the NE Pacing Derby for Jimmy Jordan, defeating his celebrated stable mate Dotties Pick and other select feature horses like Adios Harry, Widower Creed, Steamin' Demon, and Speedy Pick. In all, Dale Frost finished his career with earnings of $204,117 and joined his paternal half brother, the celebrated Adios, in stud at Meadow Lands Farm.

It wasn't long before Miller discovered that Dale Frost had but marginal fertility but still proved to be a sire of some quality, siring the likes of Meadow Skipper, Fulla Napoleon, Mountain Skipper, and Armbro Dale. Actually, if he did nothing else, siring Meadow Skipper alone ensured his place in history.

There you go, so no more putting my dad down!

Delvin Miller driving Dale Frost, the sire of Meadow Skipper

2

A Star Is Born

**"A horse—he knows when you are happy.
He knows when you are proud,
and he also knows when you have a carrot!"**

May 7, 1960
The Meadow Lands Farm, Washington, Pennsylvania

The moon was shining brightly in the sky as the residents of the Meadow Lands Farm settled in for the night. Housed in the well-kept barns were several choice broodmares who were anxiously waiting to welcome their soon-to-be son or daughter into the world.

Although it is said to be an old wives' tale, many horsemen believe that when there's a full moon, it would be good luck for mares in foal to give birth. And on the evening of May 7, the moon was almost full. Not that he needed to, but the owner of the farm, the legendary trainer/driver Del Miller, had given instructions to the farm manager, Harry Harvey, to regularly check in with the momma's-to-be. Delvin, or Del as most of his friends called him, was also the owner of the world champion standardbred stallion named Adios.

At that time, Adios was the dominant stallion in the harness racing world, if not the entire racing world. Not only was this slightly-smaller-than-normal colt at fifteen hands a well-known racehorse and contemporary of Countess Vivian's sire Kings Counsel, but he had turned out to be the ultimate ladies' man. In their racing days, Adios and Kings Counsel staged many a duel, with the King getting the upper hand more often than not.

From the mid 1950s on, however, often half of any field in major stake races were comprised of sons or daughters of Adios. The prevailing theme then was, "If you don't have an Adios, you probably won't garner much pacing stake purse money."

———◆———

Adios was actually trained and driven by master horseman Frank Ervin and at one time was owned by Harry Warner of Warner Brothers Film Studio. His pacing record at the Shelbyville, Indiana fair stood for forty-three years and would later put Del Miller's Meadow Lands Farm on the proverbial map, emerging as the pre-eminent sire of champion pacers. It was common knowledge that Miller had virtually mortgaged the farm to purchase Adios for twenty-one thousand dollars for use as a stallion, though no one could have predicted the greatness that ensued.

As his reputation grew, Adios had a very busy life as a procreator, his breeding book filling rapidly each year. From just a handful of foals in his first crop, Adios sired Prince Adios. Prince Adios was good enough to suggest that something of quality was liable to happen at Millers' Meadow Lands Farm. Adios's third crop featured Meadow

Gene, a top colt who would eventually stand stud at the original Peter Pan Farms in Ohio. Crop number 4 was one of the strongest crops any stallion has ever had. This crop featured a trio of all-time greats in Adios Harry, Adios Boy, and Adios Betty. The latter, a filly, became the first sub 2:00 two-year-old in history, while Adios Harry a Jug winner and free-for-all champ, lowered Billy Direct's all-time speed record to 1:55 at Vernon Downs. Adios Boy was a chief contemporary and outpaced Harry on occasion. Also included with this spectacular crop of 1951 were the notables Meadow Gold, Meadow Pace, Amortizor, Queens Adios, and Santo Eden. Each was tried as stallions, though none had enduring success. Still, each one had his share of stakes-winning offspring.

If that wasn't enough, Adios's 1952 crop featured a pair of all-time great mares. One was Dotties Pick, a champion race mare good enough to beat male free-for-allers, as she showed in the 1956 America Pacing Classic at Hollywood Park. The other mare was named Adora, who became a foundation broodmare at Bill Sheehan's Clermont Farm. Adoras's family still flourishes today with granddaughters and great-granddaughters in abundance now based at Kentucky's Brittany Farms.

By the midfifties, Adios was the acknowledged King of Sires, and his stature reached legendary status. One of Adios's regular bed partners, Countess Vivian, had previously given birth to four fillies, each by Adios.

These are my half sisters.

At that time, Countess Vivian was still owned by Christy Hayes' family of Columbus, Ohio. Christy adored the mare and her fillies but was hoping for Vivian to throw a colt at some point. The big mare and smallish Adios seemed to be a terrific cross, especially since her second foal, Countess Adios, was on the verge of becoming an all-time great the year Meadow Skipper was foaled.

But as it happened, in late spring 1959, Adios had foundered. It was such a severe case that the stallion literally couldn't stand, so Miller utilized the farm's other stallion, Dale Frost, to breed with the Countess. Dale Frost, a foal of 1951, like the established Adios, was also a smallish son of the emerging sire of sires, Hal Dale. Thus, the same blood cross would sustain, with a Hal Dale son on top and Countess Vivian on the bottom.

That memorable night the foaling actually took place at the Meadow Lands Farm was proof of the adage "When your best-laid plans go haywire, caution! Something quite remarkable might happen!"

And it did!

Me!

———◆———

After the night watchman made his rounds and everything appeared copacetic, he went to the office to get a cup of coffee. Whether it is a coincidence or reality, three out of four broodmares will give birth between the hours of 11:00 p.m. and 2:00 a.m. Scientists contend that the fetus, through its hormone acting on the mare's uterus, determines the time of birth. But most people who attend foaling mares believe that the mare herself is ready "when she is ready."

It was well after midnight when it started to drizzle outside. As the drops of water echoed on the tin roof,

Countess Vivian stretched out in the foaling stall and gave birth to a son. Although it was a rather easy labor and birth, the new mother may have sensed that she had given birth to something special.

A son! Finally, Vivian had a boy!

He was a handsome, good-sized colt who was born ready to make his mark in the racing world, and despite a mountain of unforeseen obstacles, that is exactly what he did! Little did anyone perceive at the time that this long-legged brown colt would grow up to be such a phenomenal stallion who would change the entire direction of breeding in the pacing world.

My mother always knew I was special!

Countess Vivian, the dam of Meadow Skipper

3

The Colt That Wasn't Supposed to Be

**"Ask me to show you poetry in motion,
and I'll show you a horse."**

May 8, 1960
Meadow Lands, Pennsylvania

The following morning of May 8, 1960, was an exceptionally warm one. As the temperature crept into the low seventies, the farmhands were busy making the rounds, feeding the hungry broodmares.

When Harry Harvey, the farm manager, made his way down to Countess Vivian's foaling stall, he was taken back. He knew she had foaled the night before, having been briefed by the crew. But Harry may have been a bit unprepared, for standing next to the mare was a long-legged brown foal, boldly staring back at him.

Instantly, Harry muttered under his breath, "Dammit, looks like a nice enough colt, but he should be an Adios, not a Dale Frost."

This brave, handsome newborn was commandingly taking his mother's full attention by aggressively nursing as only a more seasoned foal would have. Harvey sensed that this was going to be an extremely intelligent colt for he was already demonstrating his presence.

> *You're right, Harry. I was an extremely smart colt. I didn't want to share my mama with anyone. And I didn't!*

Her sturdy, exuberant newborn made Vivian a little anxious, for her previous foals, all fillies, had been even-tempered and calm. It was different this time. Baby number 5 was born to cause ruckus.

———— ◆ ————

Harry summoned the caretakers. "Come quick! The Countess has finally had a prince."

"It's too bad his dad's not Adios!"

"He's good-looking enough, but he probably won't amount to much," they all lamented in a negative chorus.

Immediately, Harry called the farm's owner, Del Miller, and informed him of this new addition to the family.

> *Who is this Adios they keep talking about? You'd think my father is chopped liver the way they're carrying on. So you think I'm not going to amount to much, do you? Hmmm, we'll see.*

Just as Vivian had given birth, one of the caretakers happened to pass by her stall. He would later comment that as soon as the newborn tried to stand on his four long, wobbly legs for the first time, it looked like he was standing on stilts.

The process of a foal trying to stand up can take hours—but not with Vivian's son! On his very first attempt, the spindly leg colt pushed his two front legs out in front of him. Then he hauled himself up so he was sitting on his haunches, looking like a wide-eyed puppy. Once again he gathered his strength and attempted to hoist up his back end and actually stand.

Oops. I guess I wasn't ready for that yet.

The newborn colt blinked, snorted, and neighed out to his mama and started the process all over again. With one final burst of energy and determination, he was up ready to conquer the world—that is, the world inside the foaling stall.

As Countess Vivian walked over to check out her newborn, the frisky colt let out a blood curdling sound that even startled her.

Laughing, the caretaker thought to himself, *Well, at least he's going to have a healthy set of lungs.*

Hey, world! Like Mr. Jolson says, you ain't seen nothin' yet!

We'll never know what Miller's immediate response was, though he had to feel somewhat vindicated hearing that the colt was at least a good looker. After all, it was *his* decision to breed that good mare to the then unproven and somewhat obscure Dale Frost.

———— ◆ ————

The very first time Del Miller laid eyes on Vivian's newborn colt, he was grazing in a field alongside his mother and the other broodmares and foals. The tall brown colt was standing several yards away in the middle of the paddock; his head lifted slightly, his ears perked, and his eyes cautiously focusing on the other colts nearby. Standing next to him like a proud peacock was Countess Vivian, showing off her firstborn son.

As Miller approached them, the colt boldly ran toward him, his wobbly legs growing stronger by the minute. "Hey, Viv, looks like you finally had a boy. I know he's not by Adios, but he's not bad-looking. Don't look anything like his sisters, but he seems okay."

As if the mare understood what he said, Countess Vivian moved closer and nuzzled her head in his shoulder. Not appreciating someone else getting his mother's attention, the dark colt slowly walked closer to the stranger.

At that moment, another inquisitive colt made his way over to see what the commotion was all about. Quickly, Vivian's son spun around and bucked toward the new little intruder, sending him off in the other direction.

"Looks like you have a mind of your own." Miller laughed. "I hope you don't give your momma too much trouble."

You have no idea just how much trouble I am going to make.

Nor did anyone else! Not even Dale Frost or Harry Harvey!

Western Hanover at Hanover Shoe Farm

4

Beating the Odds

"The horse is God's gift to mankind."

Unlike other equines, racehorses are born to be athletes with one primary function: to run fast or, in the case of Standardbreds, to trot or pace *very fast*. There are pedigree experts dubbed "masters of mating," ala the thoroughbred legend Federico Tessio and his harness counterpart Jim Harrison who spent countless hours analyzing which might be the most suitable stallion for each broodmare. That is in theory, as horses can and do make liars out of the most erudite opinions.

The generally accepted adage handed down from generations of horse breeders is "breed the best to the best and hope for the best." Unfortunately, it takes three years from the point of conception until the resulting colt or filly makes the races in order to determine just how successful this selection process actually was. Therefore, it really is a long-range gamble. Still, breeding the best to the best and acknowledging conformation and/or genetic conflicts are procedures most leading farms practice.

But every once in a while comes a "freak" from humble origins that defies all odds and displays unpredicted ability.

And perhaps, once in a lifetime, a royal flush in spades occurs—like a Meadow Skipper!

Some believe that a truly great sire will often determine what the foal will look like. This is a process called *stamping*. The truly dominant stallions tend to stamp their foals in their own image, though few may actually race like the old man. While stallions get major attention, especially in sales rings, true pedigree mavens insist that the mare—via her maternal family—will determine the ultimate ability of the offspring.

Even though Dale Frost was a then-unproven sire, the dam Countess Vivian was in the process of producing a championship caliber filly in her daughter Countess Adios. Thus, she was considered proven. Moreover, her own mother, Filly Direct, had proven to be an excellent producer, further according similar production eligibility to Countess Vivian. As it turned out, Countess Vivian's maternal extension genes were somewhat short-lived, as only her Dale Frost son proved to be her enduring generational contribution.

The odds are high in getting a colt to the races. From the moment that a foal hits the ground until he gets to the races, there are many obstacles that can occur. It's a known fact that only a portion of horses born each year will actually make it to the races. Being born with four spindly legs is only the first of many obstacles to overcome, as many need time and expert trimming in the hope of growing into a well-conformed animal. The newborn usually gets up and nurses within sixty to ninety minutes, typically after several failed attempts. On extremely rare occasions, a mare may reject her foal, thus a nursing mare must be sought out. Most farms make sure that quality nurse mares are nearby in the unlikely but real event of rejection—or worse, a foaling trauma that could severely injure the mare.

———— ♦ ————

During the first six months or so while the foal is growing and running out in the pasture with other broodmares and foals, accidents can and do occur. A colt can playfully kick another one, causing injury. Every once in a while as the colts are playing tag, one will run into the fence and get scraped up or inadvertently step into a dreaded hidden groundhog hole that can result in a sprain or a fractured bone.

In addition, after being separated from their mothers during the process called *weaning*, the foals are then put into large groups by sex and sent to large pastures to grow. Most farms will then subdivide the individuals by foaling months, so that the earlier colts or fillies are turned out together while the later foals remain with their age-group peers. Needless to say, colts can and do get rather rowdy; thus, more issues may occur with them than with the fillies.

From the time the foal is born until he goes into training at age two, the colt or filly has already been emotionally and physically through quite a bit, all of which is designed to get him or her ready for the real world: the racetrack! By training time, they've been halterbroken, have learned to walk with lead shanks, and, should they be sales-bound, have learned to stand and get looked at like gentlemen and ladies.

> *Hey, life as a racehorse ain't all that terrible. We get fed three times a day, some pretty girl usually gives us a bath every day, and we get lots of love and plenty of exercise. In exchange, we have to race once a week. That works for me.*

Meadow Skipper in paddock at Stoner Creek

5

A Change of Ownership

**"No heaven can heaven be,
if my horse isn't there to welcome me."**

Meadow Skipper and Earle Avery

1960–1961
Meadow Lands Farm, Washington, Pennsylvania

Shortly after Countess Vivian had given birth to her first colt, the Hayes family of Columbus, Ohio, sold the dam (who was now back in foal to Adios) and her weanling son to wealthy Pennsylvania horse aficionado, Hugh Grant, another patron of Meadow Lands Farm. The unborn fetus that was growing inside the mare would turn out to be another colt named Tarport Count, a decent yet underwhelming racehorse. Why the mare and foal were sold and for how much is not known, although it is most likely that the death of Mr. Hayes was the contributing factor. Certainly the fact that Vivian was back in foal to Adios probably cemented the deal for Mr. Grant.

After the deal was sealed and the mare and foal were sold to Hugh Grant, the pair remained on at Del Miller's Meadow Lands Farm. During the spring and summer of 1960, the colt "that was not supposed to be" thrived and grew. He was somewhat of an alpha in his group of young colts. Although he had decent conformation and was good-sized, Miller noticed that the colt was rather awkward and, at times, outright lazy.

One day while the sun shone brightly down on the young colts grazing in the field, something spooked them. The herd took off, bucking and galloping at a fast clip. While the colts were running in the field, Miller remarked that Vivian's colt hardly resembled his half sister, Countess Adios, that graceful free-legged champion.

"Vivian's colt is a nice colt, but I doubt that he will have half the speed his sister has. Too bad because any colt out of Vivian should be highly desirable. But being awkward and by Dale Frost are two strikes against him."

Forget my awkwardness. You have no idea what beats inside my chest. I will make my mother proud.

6

His Incredible Sister

**"The history of mankind is carried
on the back of the horse."**

Delvin Miller and Countess Adios,
the sister of Meadow Skipper

1958
Meadow Lands Farm, Washington, Pennsylvania

At about the time that Countess Vivian delivered her first
son, one of her daughters was about to win the Messenger
and Cane. Her name was Countess Adios, and she would

become the first—and only—filly to win the two legs of pacing's Triple Crown. In the opinion of many, she might have won the Little Brown Jug as well, but unfortunately, she had not been staked to the third and final jewel.

Trainer/driver Del Miller said that Countess Adios was much different than her mother. "Vivian was bigger, had a long stride, and was higher going than her daughter. Countess Adios was smaller, taking after her sire Adios, while oily -gaited and lower-going."

While nothing and no one is perfect, the result from these two superstars was a striking filly that had the grace of a swan and the momentum of a cheetah.

1958
Ben White Racetrack

In 1958, Hall of Fame horseman Jimmy Arthur broke Countess Adios for Miller at Ben White Racetrack in Orlando, Florida. Arthur's father immediately took a liking to the good-looking yearling and became her personal caretaker.

One day while the senior Arthur was out jogging, the good-feeling filly kicked the shaft of the jog cart, scraping her leg. Unable to put the hobbles on her until her wounds healed, they decided to jog her free-legged. Pleased that she went so well without the straps, Del opted to let her race free-legged, at least early on.

As a two-year-old, Countess Adios won her first few races, showing abundant promise. Shortly thereafter, the filly made an unexpected and untimely break. After Miller went over her entire body and found nothing, he probed the frog of her foot with a penknife. To his surprise, the

Hall of Fame trainer discovered a screw between two and three inches long that was lodged deep inside her hoof.

It's a wonder that my sister only broke stride one time!

The Adios filly was a pleasure to drive. She could race on top or come from behind. The only problem her driver had was she would ease up and let the lines go loose if he didn't keep after her a bit.

Hmmmm. Wonder where that came from?

Miller explained how at times she could get a little lazy, a trait that her younger brother Meadow Skipper would inherit. At the end of her two-year-old year, Countess Adios had seventeen wins in twenty-eight starts and earnings of $60,922. She got a mark of 1:59.2, which made her the second-fastest freshman filly *ever* in a race.

Messengers Stake, Cane Pace

In May of 1960, the year her brother Meadow Skipper was foaled, Countess Adios was well on her way to stardom. The filly, now three, was entered in the prestigious Messenger Pace, racing against colts held at Roosevelt Raceway.

The Messenger was the opening leg of the Triple Crown for three-year-olds. As the gate opened, the Adios colt Muncy Hanover shot to the front leaving Countess Adios parked on the outside. The tough filly was hung out to dry for three-quarters of the mile before she finally cleared little Muncy.

She then fought off Howard Beissenger's Merrie Adios, now clear, getting the golden trip behind her, benefitting from her cover. Down the stretch Countess Adios pulled away and won the race by more than a length—defeating Major Goose (Goose Bay) and Betting Time (Good Time) as Merrie Adios faded.

At this time, the Messenger Stakes had a purse of $142,786, making it the richest race in harness racing history. After the Messenger, Countess Adios shipped to Yonkers for the second Triple Crown leg, the Cane Pace.

There she covered the mile and one-sixteenth in 2:08. This set a stake record for the distance and equaled the all-age record held by older males. Once again, the Countess had decisively beaten the boys, setting fractions of 29.3, 1:00.1, 1:29.3, and 2:00.1 prior to her 2:08 finish.

July 4, 1960
Missouri, Illinois

On July 4, 1960, Countess Adios made her own fireworks at the historic track when she humbled her foes, winning by seven and a half lengths in 2:00.1. After that race, she was shipped out west where she would have to face the top colts again at Chicago's Sportsman's Park, then Springfield, Illinois, and Sedalia, Missouri.

At the Missouri State Fair, Countess Adios took a new lifetime mark of 1:57.3. She also won the second heat at Sedalia in 1:58.4, which made her the fastest sophomore ever—male or female—for two heats combined. These sizzling heats knocked free-for-all champ Bye Bye Byrd (Poplar Byrd) and the famed Ensign Hanover filly, Flaming Arrow, from the record books.

Fall, 1960
The Little Brown Jug

In September 1960, the Princess of Pacing Fillies was not nominated to the Little Brown Jug. Thus, she returned to her normal filly division, beating the redoubtable Meadow Helene (Direct Rhythm) and Romola Hanover, (Tar Heel) with miles in 1:59.1 and 2:00. In the process, Countess Adios set six different individual and heat records.

It should be noted that Romola Hanover, dam of Romeo Hanover, Romulus Hanover, and Romalie Hanover, eventually became arguably the greatest pacing broodmare of all time.

Countess Adios was so much the best of her sex that year, winning twenty of twenty-two starts, but she ultimately missed Horse of the Year honors to the mercurial Adios Butler, the previous year's Triple Crown champion and budding superstar. Now four, Adios Butler (Adios Debby— Debby Hanover) was the aged pacing kingpin and the all-time fastest pacer, via a 1:54.3 time trial record, lowering the standard 1:55 of Adios Harry set at Vernon Downs.

The next year, as a four-year-old, Countess Adios still had to slug it out with the best boys in the business. She kicked them to the curb with her biggest victory in the $50,000 HTA Pace final at Yonkers. In that race, the countess was elevated to queen status when she whipped the butts of Sampson Direct (Sampson Hanover) and Dancer Hanover (Adios). Unfortunately, for the Countess in her five-year-old racing season, she had to continue racing against the best boys that were now full-grown men.

Taking a Risk: Switching From the Pace to the Trot

When Countess Adios was six, trainer Del Miller got tired of chasing the boys, and a lightbulb went off in his head. He got an idea that he hoped would pan out. Miller remembered that as a youngster, the free-legged filly could trot a lot. At times, she would trot into position behind the starting gate before changing into a pace.

In 1963, at the age of six, Countess Adios returned to the races as a maiden trotter. Although she wasn't as prolific a trotter as she was a pacer, she did win the Chicago Trotting Derby and took a mark of 2:01.2. This set a new track record for trotting mares that was previously held by the great Rosalind (Scotland).

As it has been demonstrated time and time again, great race mares do not always become great broodmares. This was the case with the Countess Adios. During her broodmare years, she had five foals—all fillies. Her best offspring was Armbro Penny by Tar Heel (a foal of 1972) and thus a contemporary of Silk Stockings and Tarport Hap, neither of whom she could remotely approach. As a freshman, Penny got a mark of 1:58.3 and became the fastest daughter of Countess Adios, but perhaps her biggest accomplishment was eventually producing her $500,000 winning Legal Notice son, Armbro Herman.

———— • ◆ • ————

Countess Adios's first daughter and perhaps her most notable broodmare daughter was Imperial Armbro—the dam of 1974 Jug winner Armbro Omaha by Airliner. While Countess Adios's genetics did not endure like her little brother Meadow Skipper's did, she was among, if not the best, double-gaited mare in the history of harness racing.

Okay, enough already! This is supposed to be my story, not my sister's! Let's get on telling about my life!

7

Weaning Time and the Early Training Years

"When the Almighty put hoofs on the wind
and a bridle on the lightning, He called it a horse."

Fall, 1961
Ben White Racetrack; Orlando, Florida

The summer of 1960 flew by. It was now fall and that time of year when the dams would be weaned from their semidependent yet overbearing at times colts and fillies. The leaves in the trees were turning colors, and the green grass that had once been abundant in the paddocks was now brownish. There was no sign of any clover hidden in the blades of grass for which the horses would eagerly seek. The broodmares and foals started growing light fur coats to help keep them warm for the coming winter months. Dozens of colts and fillies were growing into hopeful champions. At the Meadow Lands Farm, it was weaning time.

Although veteran Harry Harvey had been doing this for years, he was always apprehensive at this time of year for the wailing fillies and colts were hard to take, even for a man's man. With the cool air and hormones kicking in, a few of the rambunctious older colts playfully tried to mount their mothers and playmates.

Countess Vivian's colt was extremely attached to his mother. While being turned out in the paddock next to the foaling barn, the insecure colt never strayed far from her side for too long. There appeared to be an invisible barrier, known as the "mom zone," a small circle around the mare within which the foal felt safe. After several weeks, the perimeter extended further away from the mare. If the foal was suddenly spooked or felt threatened, it would come screeching back to his mother.

As the weeks extended into months, the circle grew, and it wasn't long before Vivian's foal—being curious and energetic—began cavorting with other colts. The Dale Frost colt befriended a trotting bred colt by Rodney, and the two would chase about on the hills. Miller believed in allowing his foals to rough it out on his farm's rolling hills, which he was convinced helped develop strong and sturdy legs.

When his energy was expended, the colt would find his way back to his mama always nearby grazing, only to collapse and fall into a deep sleep while protected by his ever-vigilant dam. Although the fillies were somewhat less spirited than their counterparts, it was definitely time to separate all the mommas from their babies. That fall, Vivian's foal and the others at Del Miller's farm were weaned from their dams.

———— ◆ ————

Miller's Meadow Lands Farm was a grand and picturesque estate. A long, tree-lined lane led to the heart of the property. Sprawled out across the dirt road were many paddocks and barns, spaced far apart from one another so the youngsters could not be seen or heard by their only-too-willing-to-wean dams.

Countess Vivian's son did not take too kindly to the separation process. The rapidly growing colt bellowed a trifle more than his playmates did. You could say that Vivian's son certainly was a momma's boy!

Although Vivian loved her son, she was more than ready to have him weaned for she was once again in foal. By that time, the band of colts had grown more independent and spent most of their time together running and kicking up their tiny hooves and eating grass, as nature has always intended.

———— ◆ ————

The total weaning process at the Meadow Lands Farm happened over a week. Every day, several mares were taken from the herd and moved to distant paddocks until the foals were completely on their own. Then they were subdivided by sex and foaling months and placed in their own expansive yearling paddocks. By the time the colts and fillies were weaned, most of them had been given names that they would be known as for the remainder of their lives.

Countess Vivian's colt was given the name Meadow Skipper; he was named by his original owner, Christy Hayes, and farm owner Del Miller. His name was derived from the fact that Christy's son was nicknamed Skipper. Moreover, most foals that were born at Del Miller's farm were called Meadow-something or the other. Since it was Mr. Miller's idea to breed Countess Vivian to Dale Frost, Hayes and Miller collaborated on the name.

———— ◆ ————

Like young children who have abundant energy and not a care in the world, the frisky yearlings (especially the colts) would occasionally spar like young titans preparing for an upcoming match. One of the farm's caretakers who attended to Meadow Skipper as a youngster remembers him more as "a strong, silent type who could retaliate if bothered." He also commented how the colt would sometimes fly through the paddock— choppy gait and all— and then come skidding to a halt at the gate. "Even back then I thought he might be more than 'just an ordinary Dale Frost colt,' but I never dreamed he would grow into being what he was."

During the fall and throughout the spring of 1961, the band of colts and fillies at the Meadow Lands Farm grew like wild weeds. Some were broader while others towered over their playmates. By this time, their personalities were established. Several of the colts and fillies were easy to handle and gentle as lambs while others were frisky as young wolf cubs.

Meadow Skipper, who was among the farm favorites, was good-sized, had decent confirmation, and was rather handsome. Out in the field, Skipper was never any trouble; but when ot was time to bring him back into the barn for some trimming, he could be a handful.

"Seems that Skipper has a mind of his own, and when he doesn't get his way, he sulks," Harry said one day to his boss.

"That's not a good thing for a racehorse. Hope he doesn't do that on the track," Miller said. "I don't have much patience for sulkers."

I don't sulk. I'm introspective. You forget I have a breed to impact. Actually, you really couldn't know that at this point.

1961
Ben White Racetrack; Orlando, Florida

The fall of 1961 was a crispy and cool one. Del Miller was busy separating the selected yearlings that would ship to the Harrisburg Sale from the others who would head south to Ben White Racetrack. Each fall, the best of the best in harness racing called the training center on Lee Road in Orlando, Florida, home. Among them were legends Stanley Dancer, Billy Haughton, Clint Hodgins, Del Miller, and John Simpson.

———•———

Ever since Meadow Skipper was born, Miller paid close attention to the colt. Because of the success of his sister Countess Adios, he figured best to give the colt a chance to see if he had what it took to be a good racehorse. Heck, if he were only half as good as Countess Adios, everyone would be happy.

Miller called the colt's owner Mr. Grant and told him, "Can't promise he will be a good one like his sister, but we'll give it a shot. Actually, I'll have Jimmy Arthur, who got his sister going, start with him.

> *I don't even know my sister, but don't sell me short, Miller.*

———•———

In the fall of 1961, the lanky youngster took the long truck ride south as part of the Miller Stable contingent. The trip from Washington, Pennsylvania to Orlando, Florida was a long and grueling one for the occupants on the trailer, especially since not all of the interstate highway system was complete.

The anxious colts were closely watched by grooms who stayed with them in the trailer. They would stop every so many hours to offer them water and stretch their tired legs. As the horse trailer pulled into Ben White Racetrack, the change in climate was felt by all. It was noticeably warmer and muggier that it had been in Western Pennsylvania.

The racetrack at Ben White was a red one-mile clay track, surrounded by palm trees and green grass paddocks where the horses would take turns being turned out in. After about a week of the yearlings settling in, the anxious trainers began to acquaint the youngsters to the harnesses and bridles.

By the time the last colt was broken, there were some shattered bikes and splintered shafts lying around the barns. Several of the colts would display bruises or scrapes they sustained from a shaft kicking incident. The more stubborn ones were harder to break. Not only were they kicking the bike shafts, but several actually flipped over while hooked to the cart.

Meadow Skipper had not been a problem to break, but he didn't take all that kindly to the daily regimen. He took his lessons with repose and responded well, but he fell behind his classmates when sidelined in February due to a minor setback. By the end of spring training, Skipper seemed capable of pacing as much as the others, but by the way he went about it wasn't very encouraging.

Perhaps the most perceptive winter training reports to appear in recent years were the dispatches from Orlando written by Dr. Don McMahan. Annually, Dr. McMahan selected the top prospects after watching them all winter at Ben White. When McMahan put together his 1962 "Most Likely to Succeed" list, Meadow Skippers name was conspicuously absent.

But then again, Meadow Skipper was not a member of the A training sets in the Miller stable. About a month after he started jogging, Miller noticed that the colt would sulk and at other times was just plain lazy.

> *I'm not sure what the heck you mean, but I'm not crazy with this routine you have me on. And guess what, I really do have a future to contemplate."*

Skipper was anything but a standout especially in early training, though he had inherited his sire's long, sweeping gait.

"If your sister wasn't as good as she is, I think I'd ship your butt back home to a sale," Miller said to the colt one day.

> *I am getting sick and tired of hearing about my sister. And if you want to ship me back, that's okay with me. I'd rather be running in a field eating grass than going in circles around this track every day.*

8

Go West, Young Colt

"A horse is like a best friend. They're always there to nuzzle you and make your life a better place."

Meadow Skipper and Earle Avery at Hollywood Park

1962
Lexington, Kentucky, California

The start of Meadow Skipper's racing career was routine in terms of growing pains. After the two-year-old left Ben White Raceway in Orlando, his trainer had his upcoming racing schedule laid out.

"He couldn't get out of the gate very fast and just didn't seem like one of those good early-speed colts," his trainer said.

Skipper's first fling at competition came on May 8, 1962, at the Red Mile in Lexington, where spring racing was a novelty at that time. He wound up fifth in a 2:11 qualifier, an inauspicious start even by 1962 standards. The next try was even worse: he finished dead last in 2:14. Eventually he won a two-year-old baby race there in 2:07.2. At that time, Meadow Skipper was considered "just an average colt."

———— ♦ ————

Former USTA executive vice president Bill Hilliard drove Meadow Skipper in his first two starts.

"He just wouldn't go up to the gate," Hilliard said. "He started way back of the field, but showed me tremendous speed at times during the mile. The problem was he had to come from ten lengths off the field."

———— ♦ ————

In that era, prior to the extensive stakes program we have today, colts bred by Ohio residents could compete in state-funded races. For that reason, Meadow Skipper spent much of his freshman season in the Buckeye State, touring such fairs at Mt. Vernon, Bucyrus, Urbana, Springfield, Greenville, and the Ohio State Fair in Columbus. During that time, Meadow Skipper was driven most of the times by driver Paul Criller, though Miller finally got back behind the lines at Lexington.

After seeing a slight improvement in the colt, Miller felt that he had shown enough to send him with some other colts to California with trainer Foster Walker—that is, with slight reservation. If the aggravating sulking and laziness persisted, gelding the horse was in order. Actually, by the end of his freshman year, his statistics didn't look all that terrible, though it was understood the prevailing brain trust wanted him gelded.

What sulking? I told you I'm introspective.

October 30, 1962
Ohio

Long before Del Miller had a chance to sit behind and evaluate him in Lexington, Meadow Skipper was shipped to Northfield Park near Cleveland, Ohio. There he started in the Great Lakes Pace but was involved in an accident and didn't finish.

It was his first look at a half-mile racetrack, and one might be excused for believing that it portended a lifetime of bad luck on the twice-around ovals. However, showing the implacable disposition and the fighting spirit that eventually characterized his career, Meadow Skipper bounced back from the accident and won ten of his next eleven starts.

They called me the equine Rocky, so of course I had the fighting spirit.

In all, at two, Skipper had won a total of thirteen races, primarily on the Ohio fair circuit, not the "Roarin' Grand" Circuit, where the major stakes colts would be found. Most of the Ohio victories came on the half-mile tracks that he was uncomfortable with, given his total inability to leave the gate. He did, however, win a heat of the Challenge Stake at Scioto Downs.

———— ◆ ————

There are contrasting stories about this "imminent gelding," but while under trainer Foster Walker's tutelage in California, Skipper wound up winning an overnight race in 1:59.4. Actually, Delvin Miller had called that morning to advise Walker that the next bunch of Dale Frost yearlings were set to sell at Harrisburg the following day and that a good performance by Meadow Skipper would favorably impact their sales prices.

Well aware of this pep talk, driver Joe Lighthill took the matter into his own hands. During the race, Joe really got after the lethargic youngster on the final turn, winning in the season's record of 1:59.4

Placated, Lighthill commented, "As soon as I hit him, he perked right up and went on, but when I let up on him, he eased off. I had to make him go."

Oh, so that's what you want me to do. Win races! You'd never know it with all these repetitive training sessions in which we seemed programmed to always reach the wire together. Somebody should have explained this a little better to me.

The date was October 30, 1962. This would be Skipper's final start of his two-year-old racing season. He was now a coseason's champion with Overtrick (Solicitor-Overbid), who would be accorded honors of "Two-Year-Old Pacing

Champion." Overtrick also held the title of the fastest on the half-mile track, winning in 2:01.3 at Delaware.

Again, the stories—mostly third and fourth hand—were contrasting about his appointment with the vet, but after his season's record-equaling victory was properly digested, it was decided to leave him as is.

Good thing!

I'll say it was a good thing. They were talking about taking away my manhood! Guess you can say I owe my legacy to Mr. Lighthill.

9

A Change of Hands: From Miller to Avery

"A horse doesn't care how much you know until he knows how much you care."

Meadow Skipper winning the Commodore

Meadow Skipper and Earle Avery

1963
East Coast

Still entire, Meadow Skipper remained in California at Delmar to prepare for his three-year-old season. Back then, western harness racing would conclude at Hollywood in late November then resume at Santa Anita in early March. Before shipping east, Skipper defeated stable mate Meadow Russ in a $10,000 three-year-old event in 2:01.2.

Prior to the race, new driver and Hall of Famer Joe O'Brien was briefed on Skipper's lethargic tendencies from trainer Foster Walker and former driver Joe Lighthill. O'Brien tried to shake some life into the colt scoring down, but "he was the laziest darn colt I ever saw," O'Brien said. As they went to the gate, Meadow Skipper lagged well behind the others. O'Brien started hollering to shake him up to no avail.

Mr. O'Brien, it's not that I'm being insubordinate, but we spent the entire winter down at Delmar finishing at the wire nose to nose, so what do you expect? We're creatures of habit, and we were taught to finish together at the wire.

Jigglin' Joe, as O'Brien was often called, decided to rev him up early by grabbing the lines in one hand and providing a solid whack on his stifle, inadvertently hitting a rather "delicate" area. Startled, the colt hit the starting gate, not once but twice, yet had the lead before the first quarter, winning handily.

Delicate area! Damn right it's delicate. You almost changed the future of harness racing.

Thereafter, Skipper and the other members of the Pacific-based group shipped back east, stopping first at Michigan's Hazel Park. There, he won one of the three starts, beating Next Knight (Knight Dream) and Pole Adios (Greentree Adios) in 2:03. Then it was on to Maryland's Rosecroft Raceway, a half-miler where he won a $5,000 overnight race in 2:05.

Next, Skipper was shipped up to Brandywine, then a half-mile track, for a $20,000 early closer against "Roarin' Grand" opposition. In that race, he wound up a disappointing seventh, behind Country Don, (Adios Boy) Sly Yankee, (Tar Heel) Uncle Alex (Adios Boy), and others.

Oops. Guess I wasn't ready for prime time yet!

From there, it was back to Hazel Park where he defeated the good Greentree Adios filly, Glad Rags. After Hazel

Park, it was on to Roosevelt for the Commodore stake and another attempt with the best in his division.

On Tuesday, June 11, Vivian's first son won the Commodore elimination with a brilliant "come from the clouds" stretch rally in 2:01.2, defeating Country Don (Adios Boy) and Marson Hanover (Hoot Mon) over Roosevelt's half-mile surface. Four days later, he won the final in 2:01.4.

Suddenly Meadow Skipper was big-time!

> *Big-time is an understatement! Give credit where credit is due. I was the New Kid on the Block!"*

This set the stage for his transfer of ownership to Norman Woolworth and new trainer Earle Avery. It seems Earle was at Roosevelt for the Commodore and was duly impressed with his three-year-old improvement, having seen him in Ohio the year before.

Avery wasted no time and called his owner Norman Woolworth in Maine, saying, "I got a horse for you to buy."

Mr. Woolworth was taken aback, for during their ten years together, Mr. Avery had never asked Mr. Woolworth to actually buy a horse that was already racing. Actually, he had probably dissuaded Woolworth from buying a hundred horses.

The two men had been together for a decade and raced many top horses, including American Pacing Classic winner Hillsota, Egyptian Princess, Muncy Hanover, Bright Knight, and Porterhouse; but those were either homebreds or had been purchased at a public auction.

Up until that time, Woolworth had not actually heard of Meadow Skipper; but after Avery's persistent prodding, he contacted Hugh Grant. Soon after, a deal for a still-undisclosed amount that was rumored to be in the vicinity of $150,000 got worked out.

Woolworth recalled the anxiety he felt when Grant called him the next day. He said, "I think my hands were shaking so hard when I picked up the phone."

Norman Woolworth may not have known it at the time, but most likely that day, he made one of the best—if not the best—investment in his life.

In his first official start for Woolworth, Meadow Skipper encountered traffic problems and finished fourth in the Reynolds Memorial at Buffalo Raceway. It had been rumored that the sale actually took place prior to the Commodore Final, but the horse raced in the colors of Mr. Grant.

When Mr. Woolworth asked his trainer how he liked the new acquisition, he replied, "No, I didn't like him at all."

> *I think this was the aha moment and probably my turning point to please my new management team, but with the traffic at Buffalo, I had no shot.*

———◆———

After the Reynolds, Avery told Woolworth that he would like to try leather hobbles in his next race to aid the colt's' gait, as he seemed to be okay with them in his training miles. Thereafter, Meadow Skipper showed steady improvement and was headed toward what would be called the Climatic Cane.

———◆———

Throughout his racing career, because of his lack of gate speed, Meadow Skipper was handicapped and had to race outside in many of his miles, especially on half-mile tracks. These grueling trips eventually caused wear and tear on his overused legs, resulting in the painful splints that would plague him for the rest of his career. Today, splints are not a big deal, owing to the technique of freeze firing, but back then they could really hinder a horse.

Those damn splints hurt like hell! Especially the one on my left front that got under my tendon!

10

The Climatic Cane

"I've often said that there's nothing better for the inside of a man than the outside of a horse."

The Climatic Cane; Meadow Skipper and Overtrick

1963
The Climatic Cane Pace Yonkers Racetrack

On Thursday, September 12, 1963 (yes, they ran big races on Thursdays back then), a field of twelve gathered at Yonkers Raceway for the William H. Cane Futurity, the first leg in the "Triple Crown of Pacing." The 1963 Cane was the richest harness race in history, with a purse of $163,187. This day would be the start of the Rocky Balboa vs. Apollo Creed battle, as this was when Meadow Skipper would again encounter the mighty Overtrick.

———————◆———————

Despite drawing post 12, Overtrick was installed as the even money favorite, followed by the improved Meadow Skipper who had post 7, at odds of seven to two. The rest of the field was comprised of divisional stalwarts: Chapel Chief, James B Hanover, Fly Fly Byrd, William Time, Rex Pick, Sly Yankee, Meadow Russ, Steady Beau, and Armbro Dale. The diminutive Timely Beauty was the lone filly in the field. Missing from the group of "the best of the best" was the Canadian Comet, Country Don.

Meadow Skipper had defeated several of these foes the week before in a three- to four-year-old invitational in 2:01. But back in late June, Skipper had suffered double heat defeats to Overtrick in the Battle of Saratoga Raceway in 1:59.3 and 1:59 flat. In the latter heat, Meadow Skipper placed third behind Overtrick and the absent Country Don.

> *Something tells me this is big. I see pretty much the same cast of characters that I beat last week, but the feeling is so much more intense. It's almost like static electricity.*
>
> *Jeez, there's a lot more horses in this post parade... And yep, there they are again: Overtrick and John Patterson. I know: it's Mr. Overtrick to me.*
>
> *Look sir, you whupped me pretty good at Saratoga, but that was over two months ago, and some things have changed since then. I'm a little bigger now— stronger too—and I suspect this old guy steering me ain't afraid to demand when the time comes. You see, I'm used to these hopples now and can actually get out of the gate just a little bit.*

Damn it! I have an outside post position. What, are there twelve of us on this half-mile track? Lots better last week with just eight of us.

Okay, Mr. Overtrick, where are you? Second tier? Oh well, I'm getting parked for sure, but you will have to wiggle through traffic, and with twelve horses at Yonkers Raceway, the first turn will look like the Deegan at rush hour.

Wonder why they were knocking my father so much? There are two other Dale Frost colts in here. The big bay over there is Chapel Chief from Queen Chief, and that inbred gritty little daisy cutter Armbro Dale from Meadow Orchid. Shoot, there's no other sire that has three sons in this race tonight!

I hear him. The marshal calls the pacers. Don't know what he actually calls us, but the gate is starting to roll.

C'mon Earle, turn me already. Hey Mr. Overtrick, you ain't beating me so easy!

"Around the turn, ready for the start of the Cane Pace, it's the first leg of the Triple Crown.

"And they're off!

"James B. Hanover and Chapel Chief go for the lead. That's William Time and Armbro Dale in the middle of the track, and Meadow Skipper on the far outside," the announcer said.

Avery shoved his horse away from the gate as fast as the lethargic leaver could pick his hoofs up and put them down, going three wide into the first turn.

What! I'm leaving? I mean I'm trying to leave, but you know me and the gate ain't exactly best buddies.

Now I'm two wide, three wide around horses... nowhere near the lead...just lumbering on that turn.

I can't see Overtrick. He must be buried on the rail. That's good, I think.

Okay, we straighten down the backstretch. I know I'm three wide moving past horses, but there ain't no way I'm clearing the lead until way past the quarter pole, if at all, the way they're going!

"Approaching the quarter pole and Chapel Chief has the lead in 29.1. That's James B Hanover sitting second with Armbro Dale moving up in close pursuit third.

"Meadow Russ is on a break, Meadow Skipper now on the far outside, and Overtrick off the rail, right behind."

Going to the quarter pole and my idiot stablemate Meadow Russ makes a break, making room for Overtrick to get out!

Overtrick veers off the rail and slips in behind me. Shoot! I gotta give him cover now, and we ain't even hit the second turn!

Now we're into the turn and I'm still three wide!

Jeez, Earle, take it easy on me! Overtrick is right behind me now, looking to go four wide as we enter the stretch, and hey—shoot—we are motoring!

"Into the stretch the first time, it's Chapel Chief and Armbro Dale, head and head—James B Hanover sitting third. That's Meadow Skipper three wide and Overtrick four wide charging at the leaders.

"At the half-mile pole, it's Overtrick by a head over Meadow Skipper…That's Armbro Dale third, Chapel Chief fourth.

"Armbro Dale's on a break! The half in fifty-nine flat!"

We're into the stretch the first time, and Earle is demanding I go. I hear Patterson chirping at Overtrick. We are flying to the half in fifty-nine.

I'll clear the lead before the half-mile pole, but damn it, Overtrick wants it too!

We're even. He's got a head by almost a half-length. Here comes the turn. Get behind me, you critter. You ain't going by!

Around the third turn, Overtrick strategically ducks in behind me. Smart move, Mr. Patterson.

He has my cover again! He's in the pocket. No, Earle, I am not thinking of stopping. Let the battle begin!

Now we're approaching the three-quarter pole. Where is everyone?

Holy Toledo! The Trick and I have opened ten lengths on the rest of the field, and it's strictly a two-horse race from here. We're at the three-quarters in 1:28.1!

Rounding the last turn, I hear more chirping. Patterson's yelling at Overtrick. He's clear on the outside now.

Earle is whipping me like he's never whipped me before. Guess what, man? I ain't stopping!

In the stretch, Overtrick surged wide, but the stubborn Meadow Skipper wasn't about to quit.

No, quitting was not in Skipper's repertoire. At the wire, Meadow Skipper had a three-quarter length margin on Overtrick in a stake record of 1:58.4—only a tick off the world record.

Down the stretch, Overtrick's desperately trying to close the gap, but I got something left!

He's not gaining much at all. We're under the wire.

Probably feeling like Rocky Balboa did the first time he beat Apollo Creed, the proud colt let out a loud whinny.

Yo, Vivian, I did it! I beat the unbeatable foe! Look at the time— 1:58.4! I equaled the track record that was held by a real free-for-aller, Speedy Pick!

Hey, Overtrick! We can beat Free-for-allers! Don't know if any three-year-old has ever won faster than 2:00 here on this track, and here we just broke 1:59!

What's that you're saying? So you think you're gonna get me at Delaware next week, do you? The Little Brown Jug, huh? You're on brother. I'll see you in Ohio, but I gotta go now. You see, my fans are waiting for me in the winner's circle.

After the race, driver Earle Avery said, "I wasn't worried at any point, even when I saw Overtrick coming at the half."

In response to a reporter's inquiry chorus of "Why not?" Earle opined, "Because I knew all along I had the best horse."

Hey, Mr. Avery, why didn't you tell me you thought we were the best? I had no idea until maybe halfway down the stretch.

Overtrick's driver John Patterson felt that what beat his colt was avoiding the breaker and the huge move from the second turn to the half-mile pole.

"I had good position early, but when I saw Avery heading for the top, I yanked out after him. That took too much out of my colt." He didn't say what might have happened had Meadow Russ not made that break, allowing him to steer Overtrick from being possibly boxed in along the rail.

Immediately after the race, there was stunned silence, and all bedlam broke out. Many of the 24,066 in attendance were arguing with each other over what they just saw and which horse might have been better than the other. In 1963, there were no postrace replays; thus, it was impossible to verify what one perceived to have seen. Many in the crowd gathered around the acknowledged "opinions" to hear what these so-called learned players actually saw.

The tote board showed Meadow Skipper paying $8.70 to win, $3.40 to place, and $2.80 to show. Overtrick returned $2.90 to place and $2.60 to show, while the diminutive Timely Beauty returned $8.90 to those who bet on the mare to show.

With his winner's share amounting to $89,753.13, Meadow Skipper had in effect won himself out from his rumored purchase price of $150,000 and now loomed the third member of what eventually would be dubbed the "Terrific Trio," along with Overtrick and Country Don.

A terrific threesome! Like the Three Stooges? More like the three Musketeers, I'd say.

The Little Brown Jug

11

On to Delaware

**"No hour in your life is wasted
that is spent in the saddle."**

September 1963
The Little Brown Jug; Delaware, Ohio

Next on the agenda would be the multiple-heat Little
Brown Jug at Delaware's saucer-shaped half mile,
acknowledged to be the fastest half-mile track in the world.
Unlike thoroughbreds, standardbreds have been known to
race several heats on a single afternoon. That practice was
much more in vogue in Meadow Skipper's day than it is in
today's racing.

In order to win the Little Brown Jug—then the most
coveted event for three-year-old pacers—a horse had to
win two heats. If there were two different heat winners,
the field would then come back for a third heat. If neither
of the previous heat winners were victorious in this heat,
the three heat winners would come back again in what
was called a "fourth heat race-off" to determine the Little
Brown Jug champion.

*Three heats! That sounds like torture! Oh, my aching
splints!*

A total of ten colts and one filly converged at Delaware Ohio for the first heat of the Little Brown Jug. Most of the same characters that were in the Cane came back for the Jug. The race was comprised of Cane winner Meadow Skipper, runner-up Overtrick, Sly Yankee, Diamond Sam, Meadow Russ, and Chapel Chief. Harry's Laura, a big Adios Harry-Steinway mare, replaced Timely Beauty as the only mare to challenge the colts. Also on hand and the first heat favorite was the Canadian comet, Country Don, in post 2. Country Don had previously beaten Overtrick in their last encounter at Liberty Bell Park.

Since the "Super Horse" (as Overtrick was called) had now lost two in succession and was starting in the second tier at post 9, he was third choice on the board. Second choice was Cane winner Meadow Skipper in post 3.

Hmmm. This is even bigger than last week at Yonkers. The Little Brown Jug is considered the ultimate prize, and I suspect I'm not gonna catch anyone napping this time around. I don't think anyone, especially Overtrick and Mr. Patterson, were ready for my unveiling last week. I can still see the shock on their faces when they couldn't get past me. Now they know I'm a serious adversary.

In addition, Country Don is here, and from the two hole, he represents a whole new kind of challenge. The Trick has post 9 in the second tier, but since the rail horse Diamond Sam has all sorts of early speed, Trick will most likely get away in good position.

I've got the three hole, and I'll probably be stuck out there awhile. Of course I could always keep Overtrick boxed in, but that means getting parked the mile and then neither of us will be able to catch Country Don.

The early speedster Diamond Sam had the coveted rail position and, as expected, would set sail for the top.

As the ten horses lined up behind the gate, the announcer bellowed, "They're off. Diamond Sam and Country Don are head and head for the lead. Chapel Chief the Cane pacesetter is third on the outside with Overtrick in behind Diamond Sam now fourth. That's Meadow Skipper on the outside fifth, followed by Meadow Russ sixth at the rail."

Outside again? Hey, Mr. Avery, don't you know the rail is the shortest distance between two points?

"At the quarter in twenty-nine, it's still Diamond Sam and Country Don head and head, Chapel Chief outside third, Overtrick on the inside fourth. Just before the second turn, Country Don takes over and leads by a length. Into the stretch the first time and approaching the half, its Country Don in front, Diamond Sam back to second. Chapel Chief is still on the outside now third, followed by Meadow Skipper fourth, with Overtrick on the rail in fifth. They hit the half in a speedy 57.4."

What? 57.4! We only went fifty-nine to the half in the last race at Yonkers.

"They're around the third turn and approaching the three quarter pole. Country Don has the lead.

"It's Diamond Sam still second on the rail. Meadow Skipper just went around the tiring Chapel Chief and is now third as Overtrick finds daylight and slips out in fourth, right behind Meadow Skipper.

"Look at the timer: Three quarters in 1:26.4, the fastest ever at Delaware Ohio!

"Here they come around the final turn. There are three of them across the track. Country Don is on the rail, a head in front. Overtrick is now three wide and *flying*. Meadow Skipper is sandwiched between, back to third.

"Into the stretch, Overtrick is in *overdrive*. He's pulling away by open daylight. Meadow Skipper is a length and one-quarter back second, with the tiring Country Don two and one-half lengths back third. It's another two lengths back to the fourth place finisher Sly Yankee.

"Look at the time! 1:57.1—*a new world record* for a half-mile track!" the announcer roared.

> *Hey, Trick, congratulations! You were great, but we got another heat to go.*

With the order of finish determining the post positions for the second heat, Overtrick would start from the coveted rail with Meadow Skipper in post 2; Country Don, post 3; Sly, Yankee, post 4; Max Hanover, post 5; and Diamond Sam, post 6. This time, the second-tier trailers would be Chapel Chief in post 9 behind Overtrick, along with Delightful Time and the big mare Harry's Laura.

> *Oh, damn it! With an early speed trailer like Chapel Chief, I'm gonna get parked again!*

In this race, Overtrick was installed the odd-on favorite, by virtue of his world-record effort in the first heat and the advantageous rail post position.

"And they're off. Overtrick goes for the lead with Country Don alongside second, followed by Sly Yankee third on the outside with Chapel Chief now fourth on the rail. It's Hondo Hanover fifth, Delightful Time sixth, and Meadow Skipper gets away poorly now seventh on the rail."

Oh, that's what the rail looks like. But I'm kinda way behind. Shoot! That was a terrible start by me.

"Approaching the quarter, Country Don takes the lead. Overtrick is back to second but quickly retakes command. They go past the quarter in 28.1 with Overtrick in clear control, Country Don still second on the inside. Then it's a length to Sly Yankee still parked out third. That's Chapel Chief fourth on the rail with Hondo Hanover alongside fifth. Meadow Skipper is way back at this point.

"Into the stretch the first time nearing the half-mile pole, Overtrick has a clear one-length lead. Country Don is back to second, then a length to Sly Yankee still parked outside third. That's Chapel Chief on the inside fourth, Hondo Hanover alongside fifth. Meadow Skipper pulls to the outside sixth. "Meadow Skipper has pulled three wide!"

Don't worry, Mr. Avery. Ask and you shall receive. I have not yet begun to pace.

"Around the turn, it's Overtrick still in front, with Country Don on the rail second. Meadow Skipper circling horses, is now third and moving up."

Hey, Trick, it's me again. Let the games begin!

"They go past the three quarters in 1:28.3—a breather quarter for Overtrick. Its Overtrick in front, Meadow Skipper at his flank second, Country Don right behind third. Forget the rest. The race is *right here*!"

He went 30.2? How fast did I go coming from sixth at the half? and I had to get around those stragglers. Three wide on the turn, no less!

"Overtrick quickly turns on the afterburners, opening daylight, and into the stretch has a comfortable two-length lead. Country Don now off the rail goes past a tiring, but still trying Meadow Skipper to be second. It's Meadow Skipper third. Then lengths back to Chapel Chief fourth, followed by late closing Max Hanover in fifth. Here's the time: 1:57.3! It's another world record for a second heat and the fastest ever for two heats combined."

I know, Mr. Overtrick. Revenge is sweet. You're back on top, but next up is Lexington's Red Mile, and it's a mile track, with two less infuriating turns. See ya there.

October 3, 1963
The Poplar Hill; Lexington, Kentucky

It was October 3. The crowd of anxious fans waited for the start of the first heat of the Poplar Hill Pace. The temperature had cooled some, and it was a beautiful day for a horse race, though there was a pretty stiff wind.

I haven't seen one of these big tracks since California, and that reddish clay surface sure feels good to my feet. Even my gait that they always bitch about seems much smoother on this track. Ain't no surprises here, as even Trick knows I'm a worthy rival now!

"A short field of four is assembled here at Lexington's Red Mile for the first heat of the Poplar Hill Pace. This time, three-year-old titans Overtrick and Meadow Skipper have themselves a virtual match race, having scared off most of the vanquished Cane and Jug starters, joined only by Hondo Hanover and Diamond Sam.

"Overtrick and John Paterson grab the immediate lead from Diamond Sam, reaching the quarter in 28.4. As they straighten for the long backstretch run, Avery pulls Meadow Skipper to the outside and sets sail for the top.

"They go past the half in 57.1 as Meadow Skipper takes the lead. It's Overtrick back to second, with Diamond Sam and Hondo Hanover in pursuit.

"They continue in the same order around the far turn as Meadow Skipper reaches three quarters in 1:26.1, with Overtrick right behind a very tight second."

Okay, Overtrick. Come and get me if you dare. I am feeling goooooood!

"As they straighten out for the final drive, it's a two-horse race.

"Meadow Skipper, still in front. Overtrick edges off the rail and is *coming to him*!

"Down the stretch they come. Meadow Skipper and Overtrick—they are heads apart.

"At the tunnel, Overtrick has his nose in front.

"It's colt against colt—Meadow Skipper and Overtrick, Overtrick and Meadow Skipper, Patterson and Avery—whipping and slashing for all they're worth."

Look Earle, I heard what you told the groom. I ain't done yet. He will not pass!

"They go under the wire together in 1:55.1! It's a photo finish. Hold all tickets. Another world record for three-year-old-pacing colts. Just one tick off the all-time race standard set by Adios Harry at Vernon Downs. What kind of colts are we dealing with this year? Three straight races at three different tracks and three new speed records!

"It's official—Meadow Skipper has won it! The photo shows the Skipper a bare nostril ahead of Overtrick in what was a colossal first heat of the Poplar Hill Stake. Hondo Hanover finished a very distant third, followed by Diamond Sam far back in fourth."

> *First heat! You mean we gotta do it again? Okay, Trick. Ready if you are.*

In the winner's circle, Meadow Skipper's awed but respectful owner, Norman Woolworth, graciously commented, "It is a shame that either colt had to be beaten."

Earle Avery replied, "I told the groom if I could get Meadow Skipper to the front past the quarter, he'd go in 1:55. This horse can carry his speed farther than any I've ever seen."

> *Again he tells the groom! Not me! Good thing I got ears, for when I saw the quarters flash 1:26.1 with Overtrick right at my tail, I figured we were in for Armageddon!*

An hour later, the short but extremely select field returned for the second heat.

"And they're off! Overtrick grabs the early lead with Meadow Skipper second. They coast past the quarter pole en route to a very leisurely 1:01 half, as both drivers are content to sit where they are."

What do you mean, sit content? You forget we had a firestorm an hour ago.

"Around the turn they go, past the three quarters in 1:30.1 as Overtrick instantly opens daylight. He's now in front by two lengths. Into the stretch it's Overtrick with a commanding two-length lead."

"Meadow Skipper pulls to the outside and vainly tries to narrow the gap. At the tunnel, it's Overtrick in front.

"They're at the wire! Overtrick has won it by one full length in 1:57.3.

"Look at the last quarter! They came the last quarter in 26.2—into the wind, no less."

26.2! What did I go that quarter in? I think I gained about a length in the stretch. Oh well, 26.1 ain't too shabby! When do we do this again?

12

The What-If Messenger

"You know horses are smarter than people. You never
heard of a horse going broke betting on people."

Meadow Skipper's son, Most Happy
Fella, wins the 1970 Messenger.

Next, it was on to Liberty Bell's five-eighths track where
Meadow Skipper earns a pair of second place finishes,
behind both his Terrific Trio rivals.

In the William Penn Stake, Country Don defeats
Meadow Skipper, Uncle Alex, and Fly Fly Byrd, with
Overtrick a beaten fifth. The time was 1:57.4. This is not
totally shocking, as horses coming off dual heat affairs

at Lexington in the afternoon can be a tad short in their immediate next start, especially in a cooler, northern-evening climate.

One week later in the five-horse Castleton Stake, Overtrick rebounds, besting Meadow Skipper in 1:57.3, with Country Don sitting this one out. This would set the stage for the rubber match: the Messenger at Roosevelt—the third and final jewel of the coveted Triple Crown of pacing.

> *Look, I know this is huge! Forget Liberty Bell. Whichever one of us wins this one will be crowned "Three-Year-Old Pacer" of the year. I'm ready to go for the race of my life—splints permitting.*
>
> *Hmmm, it's a lot colder here now than when I was here last for the Commodore. That's a stiff wind coming out of the west. Earle, this track is real hard right now. Not too good for my splints! Hey, there's Country Don. Didn't know he was in this one.*

"Rex Pick has post 1. Overtrick, the three-to-five favorite, will start from post 3.

"And they're off! Rex Pick goes for the lead with William Time and Overtrick, but Overtrick quickly takes command with Rex Pick back to second and William Time third.

"Meadow Skipper is *way* back at this point. They go past the quarter in 29.1 with the field in single file. Around the second turn, Overtrick maintains a one-length lead over Rex Pick, as Meadow Skipper is now off the rail, but back in sixth.

"Into the stretch, approaching the half, Overtrick has the lead as Rex Pick pulls off the rail, but moving like a freight train is Meadow Skipper.

"On the outside, Meadow Skipper is now fourth—now third. At the half-mile marker, it's Overtrick in front a length with Rex Pick and Meadow Skipper, head and head for second. Meadow Skipper is three wide!"

What the heck are you doing, Rex, you idiot? Why would you leave the pocket at this point? I could have killed us both if Earle didn't yank me three wide with the damn turn approaching!

"The half was 1:00.1! They round the third turn. Overtrick has the lead. Rex Pick is back on the rail second, with Meadow Skipper still three wide, now third!"

Hey, Earle, we're three wide in case you didn't notice, and there ain't nobody on my immediate left. That Rex Pick is an idiot!

"They straighten out and approach the three-quarter pole, and it's Overtrick by a clear length as Meadow Skipper lumbers to him!"

Hey, Trick. It's me again. Let's get ready to rumble!

"They're at the three-quarter pole, and it's Overtrick three parts of a length. Meadow Skipper is on the outside second and gaining. They're at the three-quarters in 1:30!"

"You know Skip, we might have him," Avery muttered to himself as if the horse could hear him.

"They're edging away from the field! Around the turn, it's Overtrick and Meadow Skipper.

"Meadow Skipper goes off stride!

"Meadow Skipper is on a break and dropping back to last.

"Turning for home, Overtrick has widened his lead to five lengths over William Time and Country Don, with Meadow Skipper back on stride lumbering past horses!

"They're at the wire, and it's Overtrick cruising by four or five lengths in 2:00.4.

"Meadow Skipper catches the field to finish second, followed by Country Don, William Time and Tarport Doug!"

This would be the advantage that Overtrick needed to clinch "Three-Year-Old Pacer of the Year" honors.

In the postrace commentary, Overtrick's driver, John Patterson, insisted, "I would have won, even if he (Skipper) didn't break. Overtrick had plenty left, and I didn't try to urge him from the top of the stretch home."

A frustrated but diplomatic Earle Avery countered, "The track was hard! That splint was bothering him as it has been since Liberty Bell last month, and that move by Rex Pick at the half didn't help us at all!"

The consensus in the press box was that Overtrick would have won regardless, but there may have been one or two astute grandstand observers not totally convinced.

I can't say for sure that I would have beaten him, but damn, it would have been close! Don't forget—I took that third turn three wide because of that idiot Rex Pick! Don't use the splint as an excuse. I'd have fought to the end if I could.

Hey, Trick, are you done for the season? They tell me I am! I guess I'll see you next year. You are a helluva rival, my friend, and it was an honor and a privilege to rewrite history with you. See ya!"

13

The April Star

**"A dog may be a man's best friend, but the horse
wrote history."**

It's common knowledge among horsemen that the toughest
gap for a horse to bridge is the one between his three- and
four-year-old seasons. Even though it sometimes seems
that the three-year-olds have caught up to their aged rivals
by late autumn, that is often due to the fact that the colts
have been race hardened, especially by multiple heat races.
However, it can be much different in the spring when the
now newly turned four-year-old is coming off a layoff,
having been let down in November and December.

For this reason, the Harness Tracks of America
organization created a traveling road show called the HTA
series in which the four-year-olds could compete against
each other at the various tracks until such time they were
deemed ready to enter the aged free-for-all ranks, usually
by midsummer.

Not all four-year-olds took advantage of this
protected environment. Each of the returning Terrific
Trio—Overtrick, Meadow Skipper, and Country Don—

stepped immediately into the free-for-all class and were not disgraced.

Meadow Skipper was a respectable third in his debut outing at Roosevelt on April 11 behind the seasoned Mr. Budlong and five-year-old Adoras Dream. He finished ahead of Rusty Range, Country Don, Henry T Adios, and the incumbent FFA champion Irvin Paul, now seven.

Two weeks later, on April 25, Overtook joined the fray and was a fast closing second to Adoras Dream, with Meadow Skipper back in fifth place. Next up would be the Realization for four-year-olds, with Overtrick drawing first blood, covering the one mile and one-sixteenth distance in 2:06.4, with Meadow Skipper second, and Egyptian Pride third.

As the scene shifted to Yonkers, it was Overtrick again in the World's Fair Free-For-All as Meadow Skipper, looking gimpy, brought up the rear. One week later, Meadow Skipper finally broke the ice, winning an invitational comprised mainly of lesser-level junior free-for-allers, beating Royal Rick, Irvin Paul, and Vicki's Jet.

Next was a dismal performance for Meadow Skipper as the vaunted New Zealand invader Cardigan Bay, an eight-year-old Hal Tryax gelding, validated his rah-rah press clipping, winning the mile and one-quarter "Good Time" Free-For-All in 2:31. Overtrick stayed in the barn that night but returned to trounce his four-year-old rivals in the Empire Pace, with Meadow Skipper a non-threatening fourth.

> *You know, they were right. It's tough sledding against these older guys. Not being able to leave the gate fast is a huge disadvantage.*

Meanwhile, Overtrick and Cardigan Bay staged two of the most memorable races in history, finishing whiskers apart. Overtrick crossed the wire first in the mile and one-half International Pace in record-breaking time of 3:03.2. In that one, they came the final half in a then-incredible fifty-eight seconds flat, with Overtrick on the inside and Cardigan Bay parked out at his flank.

It was Meadow Skipper's turn to sit it out that night. Then it was Cardigan Bay's turn as the big gelding turned the tables on Overtrick in the "Dan Patch Free-For-All," lowering the track record to 1:58.1 in another noses apart photo. Again, Meadow Skipper was a nonfactor, finishing last.

This is not fun, but then again, I wasn't all that great early on last year. It takes me a little longer than others to get the motor in gear.

Back again at Roosevelt, Meadow Skipper quickly reeled off two consecutive victories at the invitational level, encountering a new rival named Tarquinius.

I heard about this Tarquinius horse. They say he's something very special. A big guy—must be close to seventeen hands."

Next up would be the April Star Free-For-All on August 28 featuring a short but extremely select six-horse field.

At this point, Overtrick had been sidelined and was reportedly done for the season. Divisional leader Cardigan Bay would go off the heavy favorite with Country Don, Rusty Range, Henry T Adios, and Adoras Dream also on hand. Tarquinius was not in the April Star.

Starting to feel like myself again. This time of year must agree with me.

"They're off! Henry T Adios protects his inside post position but quickly yields to odds on favorite Cardigan Bay as they go past the quarter pole in single file. Meadow Skipper is last at this point.

"Into the stretch the first time, Cardigan Bay is in full control with Henry T Adios on the rail second as Earle Avery pulls Meadow Skipper to the outside.

"At the half that's Cardigan Bay in front a length, Henry T Adios is now off the rail second and *surging* like a runaway freight train. Here comes Meadow Skipper on the far outside. "Meadow Skipper is now three wide!"

What kind of déjà vu is this? What the hell are you doing leaving the pocket, Henry T, you moron? We both could've been killed if Earle didn't yank me three wide.

"Around the third turn, it's Cardigan Bay in front a length, Henry T Adios back on the rail second, Meadow Skipper three deep on the turn third."

Hey Earrrlllle, there ain't no one on my immediate left again. I know you think I can do these turns three wide but that's the greatest "down under" invader of all time you expect me to catch.

"Passing three quarters, it's Cardigan Bay and Meadow Skipper, now head and head for the lead. Around the turn, Meadow Skipper has a head in front. Into the stretch, Meadow Skipper is *going by.* Just before the wire, Henry T

Adios now clear on the outside brushes up to nail Meadow Skipper by a neck or so, as Cardigan Bay fades to fifth."

Shoot! I wanted to win this race! What a trip I had to go! Like the Messenger all over again, but this time I stayed flat.

Thereafter, the Awesome Black Wave of Destruction, as Tarquinius was now called by some, had asserted his supremacy over the free-for-all division, winning the mile-and-one-quarter National Pacing Derby and the one-and-one-half-mile Nassau Pace.

In the Nassau, Tarquinius and Meadow Skipper changed leads three different times before the mile marker when Skipper was forced to give up the chase, having had his tire flattened in a close lead exchange by guess who—none other than George Sholty and Tarquinius! They hit the mile in 2:01.3 and had to go around again.

In one of the all-time great racing performances, Tarquinius with George Sholty employing his patented "rock the boat" urging style, somehow held off the late bid of super closer Rusty Range, lowering the world record for the distance to 3:03.

Tarquinius and Meadow Skipper became full blown coast-to-coast rivals as the scene shifted westward to Hollywood Park for the conclusive American Pacing Classic. On a rather untypical damp and foggy October 31 afternoon for Southern California, a field of ten would contest the mile-and-one-eighth American Pacing Classic.

From the rail out, the field featured Mike Pick, Henry T Adios, Star Gem, Tarquinius, Meadow Skipper, local hero Pole Adios, Fly Fly Byrd, Thor Hanover, and Rusty Range.

The great Overtrick had long been retired, and Cardigan Bay, also done for the year, remained back east.

From post 5 and with a longer run to the first turn due to the extra furlong distance, Meadow Skipper got underway decently and actually had the lead by the first quarter, with Fly Fly Byrd parked out in second. He yielded to Henry T Adios, who in turn would yield to the now bull-rushing Tarquinius, then three wide, passing the still parked out Fly Fly Byrd on the long straightway and approaching the half.

At the half, it was Tarquinius in front, but Pole Adios and Lou Rapone had moved up to challenge, with Henry T Adios on the rail in third. Fly Fly Byrd, still on the outside and going nowhere, was fourth, and Meadow Skipper along the rail was back to fifth. At the three-quarter mark, Tarquinius put away Pole Adios, drawing out to a one-length lead over Henry T Adios, with the outside flow now fading as Meadow Skipper looked for racing room.

"Into the stretch and Tarquinius is fighting for all he's worth, but Meadow Skipper now clears. He is *airborne*."

I got you this time, big guy. Ain't nothing gonna stop me. I'm going by and sprinting clear.

At the wire, it was Meadow Skipper by two and one-half widening lengths over Tarquinius, with Henry T Adios third, followed by Pole Adios and Mike Pick. The time of 2:11.3 was just two ticks off the world record set by the great Adios Butler in the memorable 1961 edition of the Pacing Classic. In that race, The Butler, as he was called, hit the mile mark in 1:59.4, finishing the mile and one eighth in 2:11.1 for a final furlong of 11.2, undoubtedly the fastest any harness horse has ever negotiated that distance. Meadow Skipper would go on to win one more race that fall, beating many of these same rivals, including Tarquinius, before calling it a year.

If we had more mile tracks instead of all those damn half milers, I'd have won lots more races. But as it was, big Tarqui boy, you were another helluva rival.

———◆———

When it was all said and done, the year 1964 would go down as one of, if not the greatest free-for-all pacing season of all time. So deep and powerful was that division that the 1963 champ Irvin Paul was unable to win a race all year as what came to be known as the Awesome Foursome—Overtrick, Cardigan Bay, Tarquinius, and Meadow Skipper—each took turns dominating.

Meadow Skipper would race but a handful of times as a five-year-old with the splints and other ailments shutting him down. He did beat Cardigan Bay in his initial five-year-old outing, despite being parked the entire mile at Yonkers. He then broke the track record at Chicago's Washington Park, coming from dead last to be going away in a track record in 1:57.4 despite looking visibly lame. The splints that had hindered him for years were now bothering him significantly.

The race at Chicago's Washington Park would be his last hurrah! He made an ill-advised return at Hollywood Park later that fall, but it was obvious his racing career was over. Meadow Skipper had so often raced and won on sheer heart alone.

Too bad, I might have been super as a five-year-old, better than I was at four. That is, if I could race reasonably sound.

But that was not to be, and Meadow Skipper would be sent to Norman Woolworth's showcase Stoner Creek Stud in Paris Kentucky to begin his stud career.

Oh well, at least I'll get to see some fine-looking ladies down there.

PART II

Becoming a Sire and His Amazing Offspring

Meadow Skipper in his twilight years

Stoner Creek Stud

I can't say this is a tough life down here in Paris, Kentucky. The farm is drop dead gorgeous. The bluegrass is all it's cracked up to be, and my personal paddock is roomy enough to shake these weary legs and even jog at a reasonable clip. Good thing those parked-out quarters are a thing of the past, though I wonder how Overtrick is doing up at Lana Lobell?

Cardigan Bay is still the dominant aged pacer at age ten, but he'll be facing a pretty fair four-year-old named Bret Hanover soon enough. Hey Bret, I know you're the horse of the decade and the best two-year-old ever, but like me and the Trick found out, these aged guys ain't so easy to beat—especially that funny looking old gelding with the hip down named Cardigan Bay.

I heard what happened to Tarquinius—passing away a couple of months after our heated encounters. After performing the autopsy, they actually sent his knees to Cornell University for examination by the top vets. Maybe it was good for me you weren't that sound, big guy. But then again, neither was I.

So much for nostalgia. I have the rest of my life to relive those wars, but now it's time for more pleasant things—like breeding.

I now have another very important job—pleasing the ladies and changing the direction of the pacing breed, although the latter won't be apparent until many years down the road.

Hey, Mr. Woolworth you're doing your part supplying me your better mares, but the rest of the industry sure ain't giving me much respect with the mares they're sending. What am I, the equine Rodney Dangerfield? But then I never did get any respect.

14

The Next Chapter: On to Stud

"The love for a horse is just as complicated as the love for another human being. If you never love a horse, you will never understand."

Crops Number 1 and 2

Meadow Skipper's first crop was comprised of twenty-nine mares, of which twenty-six wound up producing live foals. Of those, twenty-three made the races, with twenty-one taking records. Included in that first crop were two very respectable two-year-olds: Ideal Donut (Ideal Queen-Spencer Tell) and Sir Carleton (Don't Blame Me-Faber Hanover). Both were minor stakes performers.

Meadow Skipper saw but one daughter of the preeminent broodmare sire Tar Heel that year. Her name was Tosma Way, and she gave him a fast but B-level stakes son in Windy Way. That crop also included a filly named Taps from Lights Out by Knight Star. Taps was just a moderate performer on the racetrack but later on would gain more than a measure of fame through her own terrific sons, Mr. Sandman (Overcall) and It's Fritz (Keysone Ore). The latter would gain a measure of notoriety from his epic duel with Cam Fella at the Meadowlands in 1983, on a Monday no less.

There was a colt in that crop that raced but sparingly at age two owing to stifle problems, though he did win the American National at Sportsman's Park. It was at age three that Most Happy Fella would indelibly stamp his father on the siring map. If he did nothing else, the fact that Meadow Skipper would sire Most Happy Fella would earn him immortality.

Most Happy Fella, in many ways, was Meadow Skipper's virtual reincarnation, especially in the way he appeared hitched up on the racetrack. Like his father, he was not a good gate leaver; and like his father, he was lazy and prone to taking extra steps. For that reason, trainer Stanley Dancer employed a tight hopple despite the colt's more-than-ample size. In addition, he needed keeping after with the whip, similar to guess who?

Like his father, Most Happy Fella came along in a crop that produced two other potential super colts in Truluck (Torpid) and Columbia George (Good Time). Most Happy Fella, like his sire before him, made his Roosevelt Raceway debut in the Commodore Stake. He didn't win it, as he got parked most of the way by Columbia George, but he finished a very respectable third. Some top handicappers counseled, "Reverse the trips, and it could get interesting."

In an almost uncanny flashback to Meadow Skipper, Most Happy Fella's true coming-out party was also the Cane at Yonkers. With an emphatic three-move effort, he surged past Columbia George in the stretch, lowering his father's stake record to 1:58.3. Thereafter, Most Happy Fella would win the Little Brown Jug, beating Columbia George in two of the three heats required that day. Most

Happy Fella's overall time of 5:55.2 was a new world record for three heats divided. Most Happy Fella's 1:57.3 was the fastest ever for a third heat as well.

Back then horses didn't seem to go faster each year as they do now, aided by the aerodynamic equipment, improved nutrition, and track surface maintenance. Thus, the track and world records had far more significance back then.

Between Overtrick's 1:57.1 in 1963 and Most Happy Fella's 1:57.1 in 1970, there was just one other sub 1:58 mile at Delaware—that being the 1:57, set by Bret Hanover in 1965. After Lexington and a subpar time trial, Most Happy Fella went out West to Hollywood Park, finishing a strong second to free-for-aller Laverne Hanover in the American Pacing Classic.

As Mr. Dancer would stipulate, "Most Happy Fella is not much of a time-trial-type horse, being much too lazy. Fortunately, he liked chasing horses in an actual race."

He then came back east for the Messenger. It was the third and final jewel of the Triple Crown where he came from last after being almost impeded by Ferric Hanover on the final turn, to be going away at the wire.

Look! You know all the problems I had with those half-mile tracks? So I figured I'd better send one of my sons to do what I couldn't do. Isn't that right, girl?

In what might have been tabbed an abbreviated opening crop, Meadow Skipper had sired a Triple Crown winner. In addition, Most Happy Fella was named Pacer of the Year for 1970, and he retired to New York's Blue Chip Farms to begin what would prove to be his own incredible and enduring siring career.

While Most Happy Fella was rampaging through the three-year-old division in 1970, a two-year-old named Albatross was also showing signs of impending brilliance. A smallish, somewhat blocky sort, Albatross was an absolutely sensational two-year-old, so much so that he was syndicated prior to his sophomore season. His training and driving career was turned over to Stanley Dancer.

Coincidently, Albatross was developed by Mr. Harry Harvey, the same Harry Harvey who was farm manager at the Meadowlands farm when Meadow Skipper was foaled. Albatross, the second super son of Meadow Skipper, would then be campaigned by Stanley Dancer, the trainer/driver for Skips first super son, Most Happy Fella. Thus, in his first two crops, Meadow Skipper had accounted for two all-time great pacing colts in Most Happy Fella and Albatross.

"You think maybe now I'll get some respect," says Skipper Dangerfield.

15

His Incredible Crops

"No heaven can be heaven if my horse isn't there to welcome me."

Meadow Skipper's son, Most Happy
Fella, wins the 1970 Cane Pace.

Crops Number 1 and 2

Significantly, Most Happy Fella nor Albatross were not out of what would be considered top-of-the-line broodmares, although Happy's dam Laughing Girl, from Maxine's Dream, had far better credentials than did Albatross's mom, Voodoo Hanover. Happy, as he was nicknamed, was from a modest Good Time mare named Laughing Girl and was actually rather inbred, being a 3x3 line bred to Hal Dale.

Laughing Girl was my one special gal. The first time I laid my eyes on her, she had me at her first nicker.

He also exemplified the creative acumen of his breeder, Norman Woolworth, who is still considered one of the all-time greats for naming racehorses.

Albatross, from a discarded Dancer Hanover mare named Voodoo Hanover, was also line bred to Hal Dale, but his 3x4 numbers were more acceptable to the pedigree buffs back then. Why the other colt was named Albatross is unknown, but legend has it that he was a rather ugly duckling as an adolescent. He couldn't have looked too much better as a yearling, for he was bought back for something like seven thousand dollars.

As great as Most Happy Fella was, many will argue that Albatross was even better. Of course, at age two, there was no comparison. But as their trainer once implied, Albatross may have been faster, but Most Happy Fella was definitely tougher. Suffice it to say that both were among the greatest pacers ever foaled.

Meadow Skipper's second crop was comprised of thirty-seven living foals, of which thirty-two made the races and twenty-nine took lifetime marks. While the starters per foal numbers were somewhat comparable to those of his initial crop, Meadow Skipper's second crop, in addition to Albatross, included another major notable named Tarport Skipper.

Tarport Skipper, from Meadow Betty by Direct Rhythm, was a big lumbering sort who picked up minor spoils in many of the major stakes won by Albatross. Others from that second crop included Airy Way, a full brother to Windy Way, and Jolly Roger, the full brother to Most Happy Fella. Neither were major stakes player as colts.

The crop also included a rather nondescript filly named Skipper's Mae, by the obscure N.D.Hal. Skipper's Mae, like Taps, was not much of a race mare, but she became a stellar broodmare, producing the well-remembered Eastern Skipper, amongst others.

Crops Number 3 and 4

By now, Meadow Skipper was a made stallion, though the quality of his books through crops 3 and 4 would but improve marginally, if at all. The reason for that is that crops 3 and 4 were consummated before Most Happy Fella and Albatross reached the races, so it wasn't until the 1971 breeding season that breeders had a true awareness of just what kind of sire they were breeding to.

I told you I don't get no respect. Look, you can knock me. I'm used to it, but lay off my boys please.

It should be noted that Good Humor Man, a full brother to Most Happy Fella and the last foal from Laughing Girl, would set an all-time auction sale record, bringing $210,000 at Tattersalls in 1971.

There goes my main squeeze Laughing Girl again!

A member of Meadow Skipper's crop number 4, Good Humor Man, described as an almost perfect specimen, was conceived in 1969 and foaled in 1970. By the time he hit the auction ring in 1971, the Most Happy Fella and Albatross exploits were known to all.

Respect! I finally got some respect: a sales-topper son.

However, that was his lone moment in the spotlight. Though much scrutinized while training, Good Humor Man proved not much of a racehorse and was eventually exported to New Zealand.

While there was no compelling reason for the quality of mares to improve substantially for crops 3 and 4, his actual numbers of mares bred increased. Crop number 3, conceived in 1968 and foaled in 1969, numbered fifty-two in total, of which forty-eight made the races, including two that trotted. The headliners were Alley Fighter from Nola Abbey and the good filly Decorum from Good Taste. Coincidently, Alley Fighter, an entry mate of divisional leader Strike Out and Decorum, were from dams sired by trotter Guy Abbey, best known as the sire of the immortal Greyhound. This crop would reach the races in 1971 simultaneously with the first crop of the great Bret Hanover, who drew most, if not all, the top broodmares that year.

Crop number 4, conceived in 1969 and foaled in 1970, numbered fifty-four in total, with forty-seven making the races. While breeding season 1969 would have concluded before his first crop actually raced, there must have been sufficient quality training reports to positively influence the mare number increase. The headliners were J. R. Skipper from Good Dena Gay Skipper from the Storm Cloud mare Margies Storm and the creatively named Smog from Gray Sky by Follow Up. Of those, J. R. Skipper was prominent early on, while Smog caused a minor sensation, upsetting the heralded Armbro Nesbit in the 1973 Cane Pace.

Crops Number 5 and 6

Crop number 5, conceived in 1970 and foaled in 1971 numbered seventy-three, of which sixty-four made the races. By this point, it was known that Meadow Skipper had accounted for several stakes performers in his first crop; thus, breeders at least had confidence he could get some good ones. Featured in crop number 5 was arguably Meadow Skipper's all-time greatest female performer, Handle with Care, from the Hillsota mare Lady Emily. An undefeated two-year-old, Handle with Care took her place amongst the greatest fillies of all time, earning $809,689. Late in her four-year-old season, the tough mare beat the boys in the American Pacing Classic at Hollywood Park.

Crop number 6, conceived in 1971 and foaled in 1972, numbered eighty-four live foals of which sixty-six pacers and one trotter made the races. That crop included three significant individuals in Nero from La Byrd Abbe, Meadow Blue Chip from Mary B Good, and Seatrain from Mary Brakefield. Of those, Nero was the champion two- and three-year-old of his crop and would prove to be a major siring son. Meadow Blue Chip emerged as a top race mare in her aged form, while the gelded Seatrain wound up winning the Little Brown Jug as a three-year-old in 1974. If there were any doubts about the siring prowess of Meadow Skipper, all were erased by the performance of this group.

Significantly, Meadow Skipper would now be competing in the stallion ranks with his own son Most

Happy Fella, who stood his first season in stud at Blue Chip Farms.

> *Respect! Now I'm getting respect! I don't know if I can handle this, having been the underdog for so long. I'm also seeing more delectable broodmares, though only I knew I really didn't need them. But let me say this, I'm so proud of my boy Most Happy Fella, and I'll be watching to see how he does. And I'm well aware of the conversation between my coauthor Bob Marks and Charlie Karp in which he publicly predicted that my boy, Most Happy Fella, would emerge as a milestone stallion.*

Crops Number 7 and 8

Crop number 7, conceived in 1972 and foaled in 1973, benefitted from the aftermath of Most Happy Fella and Albatross, as they were now well-known commodities. That crop numbered 101 live foals, of which eighty-five made the races. The headliners included the major stakes star and stallion son Windshield Wiper from Keystone Mist as well as two brilliant fillies, Skipper Dexter from Dexter Tar and Misty Raquel from Richelle Hanover. There was also a good colt named Raven Hanover, who later on would sire On the Road Again's chief contemporary, Guts. That crop also included the ultimate insult, as the colt from Debutante Wick was named Super Bret.

> *What am I, Skipper Dangerfield again? Why would anyone name one of my sons after Bret Hanover, especially now when it's obvious how good a stud I really am?*

Crop number 8, conceived in 1973 and foaled in 1974, numbered seventy-six live foals, of which sixty-one made the races. Undoubtedly the numbers dropped for two distinct reasons. First and foremost would be that 1973 represented the first breeding season for his heralded son Albatross, and undoubtedly, the training reports on the first foals by his other son, Most Happy Fella, were indeed glowing. That crop was headlined by his lookalike world champion, two-year-old son Jade Prince from Oui Oui Byrd, who lowered the race record to 1:54.1 that fall.

Another headliner was the brilliant Governor Skipper from Adios Governess, a stakes superstar and future stallion son. Then there was Escort from Baby Sitter, he a genetic cousin to Most Happy Fella, who wound up winning the initial Meadowlands Pace in the spring of 1977. In addition, there was the well-known Senor Skipper and Seedling Herbert, both significant winners.

Crops Number 9 and 10

Crop number 9, conceived in 1974 and foaled in 1975, numbered seventy-eight live foals, of which sixty-five made the races. At this point in time, son Most Happy Fella loomed a budding superstar stallion, accounting for two of the greatest race fillies in history in daughters Silk Stockings from Maryellen Hanover and Tarport Hap from Tarport Cheer.

> *Look at that! My replica son is as good a stud as he was on the track. Better brace yourself for my grandsons by Albatross. Escort is damn lucky B.G.s Bunny (Albatross-Brets Romance) couldn't make the second heat in that Meadowlands Pace, after crushing his first heat in 1:54.*

The headliners in crop number 9 were Meadowlands Pace winner and stallion son candidate Falcon Almahurst from Ingenue and the superfast mare Tender Loving Care, a genetic cousin to Handle with Care.

Crop number 10, conceived in 1975 and foaled in 1976, numbered ninety-seven live foals, of which seventy-five made the races. The headliners here included stallion sons General Star, Genghis Khan, Scarlet Skipper, the brilliant distaff Roses Are Red, the fast-but-crazy Crackers, and the expensive Escape Artist.

By this point, brothers and sisters to Meadow Skipper's major colts and fillies were in demand at the yearling sales, many bringing near sales-topper prices, but few, if any, ever approached the prowess of their siblings. It seemed Meadow Skipper was always seeking "different pastures" in which to bestow his next superstar.

> *Hey, look, they say the best Viagra is something new, and I'm not married to any of those ladies. There ain't a ring dangling from my halter. Let's talk about my boys. Both Happy and Albatross are great sires now.*

Crops Number 11 and 12

Crop number 11, conceived in 1976 and foaled in 1977, also numbered ninety-seven live foals, of which eighty-one made the races. Headlining that group was the long wearing free-for-aller Skip by Night from Anita Night and the super-expensive Cool Wind from Scottish Spring. A $310,000 yearling purchase, Cool Wind was but a marginal race performer, though he did contribute to the then-fledgling New Jersey Sire Stakes.

Crop number 12, conceived in 1977 and foaled in 1978, also numbered ninety-seven live foals, of which seventy-seven made the races. Headliners included stallion sons French Chef from La Pomme Soufle (another brilliant Woolworth name), Slapstick from Hilarious Noreen, Landslide from Hobby Horse Tar, Computer from Tiffy Time, plus the good fillies Liberated Angel from Angel Hair and Watering Can from Sprinkle. Also included was a mare named Ellen's Glory from Gloria Barmin, who would gain a measure of immortality when her three-year-old Direct Scooter son, Matt's Scooter, became the all-time fastest harness horse.

Crops Number 13 and 14

Crop number 13, conceived in 1978 and foaled in 1979, numbered 106 live foals, of which seventy-nine got to the races. Among the headliners were the long-wearing Mr. Dalrae from Queens Crown, who did not look anything like his Porterhouse brother Sir Dalrae. No matter what the innuendos may have suggested, Sir Dalrae *was* a Porterhouse, *not* a Meadow Skipper. Ironically, son Most Happy Fella was also falsely accused of being the sire of Big Towner when in fact it was Gene Abbe.

Another headliner was the mercurial Trenton from Tempted, who set a speed record on one of the midwestern milers. It should be noted that Albatross was a totally made stallion at this point, with Sonsam winning the Meadowlands Pace at three that year, while two-year-old Niatross won the Woodrow Wilson.

Wow! My grandsons Niatross, Sonsam, B.G.'s Bunny, Oil Burner, Tyler B, Smooth Fella, and my grand-daughters Silk Stockings, Tarport Hap, Passing Glance, and Happy Lady. I might be starting a dynasty here.

Crop number 14, conceived in 1979 and foaled in 1980, numbered 120 live foals, of which ninety-three made the races. This batch featured Triple Crown winner and stallion son Ralph Hanover in addition to Jamuga, Green with Envy, George Allen, and Flying Rich. Ralph Hanover, superior on the racetrack to his brother Raven Hanover, was probably behind his brother in the stud ranks. It was one of the few times Meadow Skipper actually sired brothers of somewhat comparable ability from the same mare.

Crops Number 15 and 16

Crop number 15, conceived in 1980 and foaled in 1981, numbered seventy-seven live foals, of which sixty-five made the races, including two outstanding filly headliners in Naughty But Nice from Angel Hair and Don't Dally from Dalliance. By this time, most observers would have ranked Meadow Skipper third amongst the leading sires, behind his sons Albatross and Most Happy Fella.

Hey, nothing lasts forever, but playing third fiddle to my two boys is fine with me.

Crop number 16, conceived in 1981 and foaled in 1982, numbered ninety-two live foals, of which seventy-one made the races. This would prove to be the last hurrah for the Rocky Balboa of Standardbreds. His last crop featured one more headliner in Chairmanoftheboard from Racy Raquel.

In all, Meadow Skipper would sire 1,267 live foals, of which 1,034 made the races, including 1,028 pacers and six trotters. By the time this final crop would make the races, Meadow Skipper's grandson Niatross (Albatross-Niagara Byrd) would send his first crop to the racing wars, including his son Nihilator from Margies Melody. Nihilator was Meadow Skipper's great-grandson, and he often raced with Meadow Skipper's last good son, Chairmanoftheboard. Niatross was considered by many as the greatest pacer ever to peek through a bridal, and Nihilator was not all that far behind. And that was just his Albatross branch.

The Most Happy Fella branch featured his own superson Cam Fella and son Oil Burner's super son No Nukes, whose produce would extend the line to where it is today. No Nukes was thus a grandson of Most Happy Fella and a great-grandson of Meadow Skipper. A third link from Most Happy Fella extended through his son Tyler B, in turn sire of Dragon's Lair and the one responsible for the still-active Dragon Again. That one is the sire of the all-time richest pacing horse Foiled Again, winner of $6,923,781 and still going strong.

What am I, a pensioner with grandsons, granddaughters, great-grandsons and great-granddaughters all over creation? Talk about senior moments. I can't keep track of all this tribe anymore. Regrets there were a few.

16

Meadow Skipper's Reincarnation His Son Most Happy Fella

"There is no better place to heal a broken heart than on the back of a horse."

Most Happy Fella at Blue Chip Farms

The Siring Sons

The enduring question to any great sire then becomes, "Is he a 'sire of sires'? Will his sons sire on and extend and expand his legacy?" Most great sires will have one or perhaps two sons that carry the legacy further, and as was documented in Muriel Lennox's superb Northern Dancer book, the rare stallion may have more.

Most Happy Fella (Meadow Skipper-Laughing Girl)

Most Happy Fella is Meadow Skipper's first great son and arguably his best, even though many will cede that honor to Albatross, from his second crop. Most Happy Fella's racing career closely paralleled that of his father as did his stallion career. In many ways, Most Happy Fella was Meadow Skipper's "chip off the old block," and it was he who would extend and enhance the sire line so that it's probably impossible to find a modern-day pacing horse without at least one Meadow Skipper cross in his extended pedigree.

From inception, it was obvious that Most Happy Fella would emerge as a milestone stallion, as his first crop featured not one but two fillies who would qualify as all-time greats. One of them, Tarport Hap from Tarport Cheer, was a large Amazon-type filly, very reminiscent of her sire in appearance. The other filly, Silk Stockings, from Maryellen Hanover, seemed a bit more feminine in appearance on the racetrack, though she was anything but dainty in competition. They raced each other dozens of times, especially in the fledgling New York Sires Stakes program, with Silk Stockings holding the edge as a two- and three-year-old.

In the middle of her three-year-old season, Silk Stockings went on a rampage, assaulting and lowering track records held by colts, including her own great sire. The highlight of her season was a 1:57.3 track record at Monticello in the RICH Monticello OTB classic, in which she thrashed the colts. Silk Stockings was named Pacer of the Year for 1975; thus, Most Happy Fella, like his sire Meadow Skipper, would account for an actual pacing champion in his very first crop. Meanwhile, Tarport Hap kept improving from year to year; and as a five-year-old, she set a track record at Roosevelt in the U.S. Pacing Championship, annihilating the best-aged males in training.

Since Most Happy Fella's major offspring in his first crop were fillies, there were those who wondered if he was destined to be just a filly sire. That was dispelled the very next year as his second crop featured outstanding colts in Oil Burner from Dottie Shadow, Smooth Fella from Smooth Talk, and Precious Fella from Precious Newport.

Of those, Oil Burner was perhaps the best pacing colt from late summer 1976. He even defeated free-for-all-caliber older males in the American Pacing Classic at Hollywood Park. In that one, he beat the champion "aged pacer of the year" Rambling Willie, affectionately known as "the horse that God loved." The reason for that was a portion of Rambling Willie's earnings was donated to a church in rural Illinois.

Smooth Fella set a track record in upstate New York then was exported down under to Australia, where he became one of the greatest sires to grace the southern hemisphere. Precious Fella eventually joined his sire at Blue Chip Farms with moderate success, his best being son Brand New Fella.

Oil Burner raced through age four, then as a five-year old was sent to Lana Lobell Farm in Bedminster, the then-preeminent New Jersey breeding establishment. Oil Burner was not a raging success as a stallion, but his first crop featured a colt from the Overtrick mare Gidget Lobell named No Nukes, who was not only a great racehorse but also emerged as the dominant stallion of his generation.

> *Hey, Overtrick, I knew we'd do something good together. No Nukes is my great-grandson on his father's side and your grandson on his mother's side.*

By now, it was quite apparent that these direct extensions from Dale Frost, via Meadow Skipper, could throw instantaneous greatness in their very first crops. Would No Nukes follow suit? His first crop featured Sweetheart-winning filly Nadia Lobell, the best pacing filly of 1985, and a colt named Jate Lobell, the champion freshman pacer of that same season. No Nukes was made! And totally unlike his sire Oil Burner, No Nukes carried on becoming the dominant pacing stallion of the late eighties and early nineties. During that span, he sired great colts in Die Laughing and Western Hanover.

It would be the latter colt that would emerge as a dominant stallion into the 2000s, siring super sons Western Ideal, The Panderosa, Western Terror, and Well Said. Of those, Western Ideal still ranks among the leading sires in the present day, with two very distinct male line extensions, one being from his great though prematurely deceased son, Rocknroll Hanover, and the other from Rocknroll's main racing rival, American Ideal.

Both Rocknroll Hanover and American Ideal were also instant successes as stallions, making Western Ideal perhaps the first stallion in history to offer two major siring sons in the same crop. Furthermore, Rocknroll Hanover and American Ideal now have impressive sons in stud, further solidifying their sire's impact on the breed.

In 1979, the same year No Nukes was born, Most Happy Fella accounted for his all-time greatest son known as Cam Fella, "the pacing machine." Cam Fella is still considered one of the great pacers of all time and, while smaller than his sire, embodied the fighting heart so reflective of his grandsire, Meadow Skipper. Cam Fella first stood stud at Jef's Standardbred Country Club in Far Hills, New Jersey, and, like his sire and grandsire, was an instantaneous hit, getting champion Camtastic in his first crop.

Next would come major sons in Goalie Jeff, Precious Bunny, Presidential Ball, Cam's Card Shark, Camluck, and Cambest. All were successful sires, with Cams Card Shark, Camluck, and Cambest proving long-term, enduring sires. Cam's Card Shark's best son, Bettor's Delight, is and has been one of the top two or three stallions in the northern and southern hemisphere over the last few years. Thus, from Most Happy Fella emerged two distinctive male line sources, one from Oil Burner via No Nukes and the other from Cam Fella via his sons, particularly Cams Card Shark.

It is imperative to note that a substantial number of today's leading colts and fillies carry this direct double male line cross to Most Happy Fella via the sons of the No Nukes stallion Western Hanover, particularly Western Ideal and Cam Fella's son, Cam's Card Shark. Thus, an American Ideal colt from a Cam's Card Shark mare (like Heston Blue Chip) is six generations removed from Most Happy Fella on his male side and three generations removed on his female side. And that Bettor's Delight filly from the Western Ideal mare (like See You At Peelers) is four generations removed from Most Happy Fella on his male side and five generations from Most Happy Fella on his female side. There's a third, though not as link extending, directly from Most Happy Fella still active in the present day. That one stems from Most Happy Fella's son Tyler B, through his son Dragons Lair, and that one's still thriving son, Dragon

Again. Significantly, the richest pacing horse of all time, the ageless Foiled Again is a son of Dragon Again.

And yet, every name in this section traces right back to me. Happy, you are even more influential than I was, and I could not be more proud.

Not to be outdone, Western Hanover's other son The Panderosa has a good siring son in Ponder, while additional sons Western Terror and Well Said have proven solid contributors to today's pacing breed. Well Said, in particular, has managed most of his better performers from Most Happy Fella line mares. There's that double line cross again.

Significantly, Most Happy Fella carried the then-fledgling Empire State breeding program on his broad back, definitively proving that not all leading, grand circuit sires needed to reside in Kentucky or Pennsylvania. If Meadow Skipper did nothing more than sire Most Happy Fella, his contribution to the breed would be *enormous*.

But I did so much more than just sire Happy. What about Albatross?

17

Skipper's Other Famous Sons

"We love horses for what they embody: freedom,
spirit, adventure, perseverance, and drive."

Albatross at Hanover Shoe Farms

Albatross (Meadow Skipper-Voodoo Hanover)

While Most Happy Fella, like Meadow Skipper before
him, tended to sire horses that would improve from ages
two to three, Albatross, true to his precocity, sired colts and
fillies that were sensational from the outset.

Albatross was a brilliant sire, eclipsing both his paternal
brother Most Happy Fella and father Meadow Skipper,

during the midseventies and early eighties. At one point, his stud fee had swelled to seventy-five thousand dollars per live foal: that is, if one could actually obtain a booking. In addition, Albatross ruled the roost at the legendary Hanover Shoe Farms and was one of, if not the greatest income-producing sires via monies received from yearling prices and stud fees.

Among the great horses sired by Albatross include Niatross, Sonsam, B.G.'s Bunny, Royce, Jaguar Spur, Three Diamonds, Fan Hanover, Passing Glance, Praised Dignity, Colt Forty Six, Conquered, Arties Dream, Jonquil Hanover, Jefs Eternity, Jambooger, Merger, Ideal Society, Cheery Hello, Turn The Tide, Fundamentalist, Armbro Wolf, Walt Hanover, etc. Of those, Niatross was generally considered the greatest pacer of his or any generation, and was even named athlete of the year in 1980 by the influential *New York Post*. Back then, harness racing was still in its heyday, and Niatross was as much an equine celebrity as any thoroughbred of that era.

One by one, the sons of Albatross hit the stud ranks. His first major one, B.G.'s Bunny, went to Apt to Acres in New Jersey and was an instant success with such as McKinzie Almahurst, Rabbit Road, Butler B.G., Allwin Steady and others in his early crops. Partially owned and syndicated by Louis P Guida, B.G.'s Bunny was given the Hollywood-star treatment with glossy ads put together by Mike Rashkow, but in the end, it didn't help all that much. Following successful early crops, B.G.'s Bunny seemed to peter out in terms of siring quality production. One of his daughters hooked up with Cam Fella to produce Precious Bunny, but in the long run, B.G.'s Bunny was not an enduring sire.

Next up was the brilliant Sonsam, who was but marginally fertile. Like B.G.'s Bunny, Sonsam started out well, getting Primus, Radiant Ruler and Hit Parade early on; but after a couple of crops, he too petered out. He left one potentially good stallion son in Marauder, who was not a successful sire. Sonsam did sire Nobleland Sam from a Most Happy Fella mare that enjoyed success in Ohio for a number of years, though Sam has not left any successor sons.

Then it was the fabled Niatross ,who via his super sons, Nihilator, Pershing Square, Niafirst, Handsome Sum, and others, produced one of the most impressive first crops in the annals of harness racing. His second crop which featured Barberry Spur, though not as glittering as the first crop, was substantial nonetheless. Niatross was then transferred from his Kentucky base at Castleton Farms to New York's Pine Hollow Stud, and from there ,it was all downhill. Back then it was commonly believed that stallions should never be moved; hence, the downgrade of Niatross was attributed to the location transfer.

In light of the plight of the other sons of Albatross, that may not be entirely the case. Some said Niatross threw ugly, poorly conformed individuals, but that would have been applicable to his early crops as well. Suffice it to say, the male line from Niatross has not endured.

Much the same can be said for the other sons of Albatross like Praised Dignity, Royce, Merger, Conquered, etc. All showed promise in the early crops, but one by one, each petered out as they went along. Incredibly, there is not one direct major male extension from Albatross currently in existence today. As it turned out, the real enduring links from Albatross came from his daughters, as Albatross proved to be one of the great broodmare sires of all time.

One of his daughters, Wendymae Hanover, is the dam of enduring sire Western Hanover. Another daughter, Miss Elvira, is the dam of Artsplace, the primary male line extention from Adios. Artsplace had several good siring sons, including one of today's leaders, Art Major, who is from a mare by Nihilator. Thus, Art Major carries a double cross to Albatross on his female side.

> *See, my boy Albatross was really a ladies' man, and if I'm not in the extended pedigree via Happy's sons and grandsons, I am with Albatross via all his daughters and granddaughters. Great job, guys. You make the old man proud!"*

It is probably one of the great enigmas in the breeding business why some stallions start out with exceptional early crops only to not sustain that early brilliance. It stands to reason that after the first couple of crops are major hits, the sire will receive higher quality mares in his middle crops. For some, it works, and the stud keeps the quality stream flowing steadily well into his later years. In the case of Albatross, it didn't happen, but the record indicates that many of the Hal Dale male liners tended toward early crop brilliance. Not that there couldn't be a great one later on; it's just that the overwhelming majority of their superstars would happen early on.

While the Adios line exists today, it stems through the most unlikely of sources, that being his son, Henry T Adios. A gifted and versatile racehorse, Henry T Adios was one of the all-time better sons of Adios, though probably not among his leading half dozen. Henry T Adios proved but a marginal sire at best, getting but one memorable performer in Silent Majority from Hobby Horse Tar.

Silent Majority himself, a contemporary of Strike Out in the early seventies, was also anything but a substantial stallion, although he did have one important son named Abercrombie. A durable race colt, Abercrombie was initially a solid sire until breeders got the bright idea to supply him with Meadow Skipper and Meadow Skipper line mares. From then on, Abercrombie became a world-class pacing sire and seemed particularly fond of mares by Albatross, getting brilliant race colts in World Champion, Artsplace, and Jug winner, Life Sign, from Albatross mares. Singlehandedly, Artsplace restored the Adios line to prominence. That is still evident today with his son Art Major being a leading sire and grandson Yankee Cruiser, (Artiscape) siring the 2014 aged pacing champion Sweet Lou. That one will get his opportunity at Diamond Creek Farms. Significantly, Meadow Skipper is well represented in the pedigree of Art Major, through his Nihilator dam, Perfect Profile.

See, all you skeptics out there! Imagine what would have happened if Mr. Miller didn't switch my mom to Dale Frost that year! None of my Adios brothers were any good as stallions, and I can be found in the extended pedigree of just about every pacing horse alive today in the northern hemisphere. Mr. Miller, you were a genius!

Nero (Meadow Skipper-La Byrd Abbe)

Nero, perhaps the best Meadow Skipper son after Albatross and Most Happy Fella, was located at Lana Lobell Farms of Hanover, Pennsylvania, and, typical of a Meadow Skipper stallion, was an instant siring success.

Nero, too, had many outstanding sons, like Icarus Lobell, Runnymede Lobell, and Trutone Lobell; but none endured as a significant stallion. Nero produced exceptional fillies like Bardot Lobell, Kala Lobell, and many others, and through them can be found in many of today's extended pedigrees. In fact, Nero is a maternal grandsire of the 2014 Pacer of the Year, Sweet Lou. Nero did not extend or endure via his male line.

Scarlet Skipper (Meadow Skipper-Adios Scarlet)

Scarlet Skipper might have been one of Meadow Skipper's better stallion sons had he not died prematurely at age ten after being relocated to New Jersey. From modest broodmares at best, Scarlet Skipper himself, a terrific two-year-old, accounted for a number of hard-hitting prospects, including Russ Lyn Scott from Goldcreek Estee in his first crop. Crop number 2 featured Forrest Skipper from Camden Caroline among the better pacers of his years. Forrest Skipper later stood stud at Fair Winds Farm in New Jersey, achieving moderate success.

Captain Courageous (Meadow Skipper-Maxine's Dream)

A three-quarter brother in blood to Most Happy Fella, Captain Courageous was but a marginal member of Meadow Skipper's first crop. He did sire one truly outstanding filly named Courageous Lady, but not much else worth mentioning.

Raven Hanover (Meadow Skipper-Ravina Hanover)

While this Meadow Skipper from Ravina Hanover had one major son in the celebrated Guts, he too gradually faded to oblivion. Ironically, he was probably a better sire than his gifted brother Ralph Hanover, but more about that later.

Windshield Wiper (Meadow Skipper-Keystone Mist)

Not one of Meadow Skipper's best racing sons, Windshield Wiper was but an ordinary stallion in stud. He got his chance at Castleton but produced few memorable offspring.

Governor Skipper (Meadow Skipper-Adios Governess)

Though projected as Meadow Skipper's successor son by less than erudite though outspoken harness scribes, Governor Skipper started out brilliantly, getting Fortune Teller, American Freedom, and Umbrella Fella in his first crop, and the superb filly, Follow My Star, in his third crop. Not the most fertile of Meadow Skipper sons, the Governor was barely used in his middle years, getting but five live foals from the twenty-five mares covered in 1986 and not one from six mares bred in 1987. None of the Governor's sons made any significant contribution in stud.

Jade Prince (Meadow Skipper-Oui Oui Byrd)

Creating a sensation pacing in a record 1:54.1 as a two-year-old in 1975, this virtual lookalike son of Meadow Skipper was anything but his father in the stud barn. Jade Prince stood for several years but, after season number four, was barely utilized.

Escort (Meadow Skipper-Baby Sitter)

The Meadowlands Pace hero and genetic cousin to Most Happy Fella remained in New Jersey at Walnridge Farm. He sired but one million-dollar winner in Perfect Out from Allwin Diva but was not an enduring stallion.

VICTORIA M. HOWARD AND BOB MARKS

Falcon Almahurst (Meadow Skipper-Ingenue)

The blue-blooded gutter fighter by Meadow Skipper from Invincible Shadow's sister Ingenue, (Shadow Wave-I'm It) was a Meadowlands Pace winner amongst other major stakes. From his home base in Ohio, Falcon Almahurst saw his share of well-bred mares and produced solid colt and filly performers like Stienam, B.J.s Scoot, Raque Bogart, and Joss. He'll show up in some prominent contemporary pedigrees via Stienams Artsplace daughter, Stienams Place, dam of Rocknroll Hanover's recent sensation, Put On a Show.

Skip by Night (Meadow Skipper-Anita Night)

Primarily a half-mile-track, free-for-all star, Skip by Night was used sparingly in Maine and New York, getting raceway-type performers. He was not an outstanding stallion.

Genghis Khan (Meadow Skipper-Robin Dundee)

Bred to be a free-for-aller from Robin Dundee—perhaps the best mare ever sent to these shores from New Zealand—Genghis Khan finally came to prominence at age six, developing into a superior aged pacing horse. However, he was anything but that as a sire. He had but one half-million dollar winner in Ali Khan, who just barely got over the number by $5,896.

Captain Hook (Meadow Skipper- Miss Blue Jay)

Captain Hook gets listed here through the exploits of his son, San Simeon—billed as the Australian wonder horse—when he came to the Meadowlands in 1982 to take on Beatcha, Genghis Khan, Skip by Night, and others in an attempted renewal of the old International Pacing Series that Yonkers used to host. Whatever San Simeon may have shown down there, we didn't see it here.

General Star (Meadow Skipper-Bardot Hanover)

From his base in Ontario, General Star sired but one millionaire in Covert Action, Ray Schnittker's New York-New Jersey mainstay. General Star was but a marginal stallion.

French Chef (Meadow Skipper-LA Pomme Soufle)

An outstanding two-year-old for Stanley Dancer, French Chef had two superb sons in his first two crops. One was Amity Chef, from Hush-a-Bye, a winner of $1,372,683, who gained a measure of lasting fame when his daughter Miss Easy took her place amongst the great pacing fillies of all time. The other son, Frugal Gourmet from Byrdlesk, upset Jate Lobell and Run the Table in the Meadowlands Pace in 1990.

Then from Sunburn in crop number 4, French Chef delivered his optimum son in Beach Towel, a winner of over $2.5 million. Beach Towel is revered for his great son Jennas Beach Boy and his daughter Where's The Beach, she the dam of an all-time great pacer in Somebeachsomewhere. SomeBeach, as he was known, was considered on a par with Niatross amongst the best pacers of the last three decades.

And thanks, Kathy Parker, for illustrating that my name appears no less than four different times in the five generation pedigree of Somebeachsomewhere.

Though he had his moments, French Chef was not a brilliant sire.

Slapstick (Meadow Skipper-Hilarious Noreen)

A contemporary of French Chef in their colt days, Slapstick from Hilarious Noreen stood at both Lana Lobell and Perretti Farms in New Jersey. Other than Grade One and Reactor Lobell (two $800,000 plus winners), Slapstick was a marginally successful stallion at best.

Landslide (Meadow Skipper-Hobby Horse Tar)

A half brother to the brilliant Silent Majority, Landslide got his chance at stud first in Indiana and later at Stonegate farms in New Jersey. He did sire one superstar in Run the Table from Hustler's Best, who became a leading sire in Canada for many years. From the Oil Burner mare, Cathedral City, Run the Table sired a wonderful race and broodmare named Cathedra, arguably among the greatest income-producing broodmares of all time.

Computer (Meadow Skipper-Tiffy Time)

From Tiffy Time, Computer had but one half-million-dollar-plus winner in the long-lasting Search Party but was anything but a stallion success.

Ralph Hanover (Meadow Skipper-Ravina Hanover)

One might definitely label Meadow Skipper's final Triple Crown winning son, Ralph Hanover, as an abject failure, but as one of his offspring, he would earn over three hundred thousand dollars. Ralph Hanover got his chance at

Almahurst, but he must be regarded as Meadow Skipper's worst siring son amongst his better performers.

ChairmanoftheBoard (Meadow Skipper-Racy Raquel)

Meadow Skipper's last major son and his final siring prospect proved anything but that as a stud. He too had but one half-million-dollar winner.

> *Oh well, you can't win 'em all, but Ralph really did shock me. I thought he would at least be average, but I agree, he was terrible.*

It could be argued that many of the Meadow Skipper siring prospects did not attract the elite broodmare consorts; but then again, neither did he, especially in those vital early years. After it became obvious that Meadow Skipper was indeed a potentially great stallion, breeders from everywhere supplied him with their best mares. Ironically, he didn't seem to need them and habitually would produce a star from an entirely unexpected source, like trotting bred La Pomme Souffle, the Nevele Pride dam of French Chef.

Meadow Skipper's Broodmare Daughters

There hasn't been that much written about "Meadow Skipper, the broodmare sire" most likely because he was obviously more superior at being 50 percent of the equation as a sire than the 25 percent he was reduced to in the second generation as a broodmare sire. This is somewhat borne out in the fact that his presence alone in the second generation was not enough to make his sons stallion stars other than the two best, Most Happy Fella and Albatross.

Both Happy and Albatross were great sires based on their ability and individuality.

> *Hey, look, Happy was more like me than Albatross was, but I know Happy's sons and daughters are more like him than me.*

In addition, many of the leading sires of that era just happened to be his sons and grandsons, rendering them genetically ineligible to breed to Meadow Skipper broodmares. Still it was tried occasionally, and it can be noted that Pershing Square, one of the better sons of grandson Niatross, was out of his daughter Treasure Blue Chip. For the most part, the Meadow Skipper broodmares were bred to what was then called the non-Meadow Skipper line outcross stallions.

Perhaps his first daughter to produce a foal was Taps from Lights Out by Knight Star, dam of one of the better Overcalls named Mr. Sandman. That Capetown brother to Overtrick was a lackluster sire at best. Other than his son Shirley's Beau, it's hard to remember another decent Overcall performer after Mr. Sandman. Physically, Mr. Sandman looked much more like his grandsire Meadow Skipper than he did his sire Overcall. Taps would later have another famous son in It's Fritz by Keystone Ore. That one was eventually tried as a stud but was marginal at best.

Arguably, the two best horses to come from Meadow Skipper mares are Matt's Scooter (Direct Scooter-Ellens Glory) and Call For Rain (Storm Damage-Rain Proof), in whichever order you'd like to put them. Both qualify as legitimate all-time greats and are by far the foremost individuals to be sired by their respective sires. Of the two,

Matt's Scooter was a successful though not great stallion, while Call For Rain was an abject failure.

Amongst the other notables credited to Meadow Skipper's daughters include Robust Hanover (Warm Breeze- Rosalie Hanover), Kentucky Spur (Abercrombie-Peach Melba), Incredible Finale (Shadows Finale-Queen Margie), Leah Almahurst (Abercrombie-Liberated Angel), Pershing Square (Niatross), Seahawk Hanover (Bret Hanover-Skipper's Romance), Eastern Skipper (Bye Bye Byrd-Skipper's Mae), Laag (Abercombie-Tinsel), Trim The Tree (High Ideal-Tinsel), etc.

Some, like Liberated Angel, were from impeccable maternal families, while others were distinctly from more modest maternal links. Still, more than one stallion realized one of, if not his all-time best performer, from a Meadow Skipper daughter. Then again, from stallion inception, Meadow Skipper was anything but predictable, as one never knew where the next star performer might come from.

That's me: Mr. Unpredictable. I'll strike where I ain't yet struck!

And that he did, as yearling buyers bid millions of dollars on colts and fillies perceived to be the next Meadow Skipper champion and more often than not were incorrect, as he seldom threw like from the same mare. Meadow Skipper was the leading sire of $100,000 yearlings through the 1983 season—the last year his crop reached the auction rings.

In all, Meadow Skipper accounted for thirty-four $200,000 plus yearlings, six of them sales-toppers, seven Cane Pace winners, five Messenger winners, and four Little Brown Jug champions.

18

Recreating the Breed in His Own Image

"All I pay my psychiatrist is the cost of feed and hay, and he'll listen to me all day long."

Meadow Skipper Today

While there might be one somewhere in 2015, it is virtually impossible to find a northern-hemisphere-based pacing horse without at least one major link to Meadow Skipper. Most have several crosses within their five-generation pedigrees, with the overwhelming majority of his male line tributaries stemming through his son Most Happy Fella. That alone is incredible, considering Most Happy Fella was put down in 1983 after siring just thirteen crops as a result of an inoperable pasture injury.

> *We were crushed when we heard that terrible news. I loved all my 1,267 kids, but like your first love, that first great one seems extra special.*

From the female side, his other sons and granddaughters get into the act, particularly those by Albatross. It may be significant that Western Hanover, perhaps the most influential sire of the two past decades, is by No Nukes, a grandson of Most Happy Fella from the Albatross mare

Wendymae Hanover. This makes him line bred 4x3 to Meadow Skipper.

In addition, Cam Fella's most successful son Cam's Card Shark is 3x4 line bred to Meadow Skipper via his B.G.s Bunny dam, Jef's Magic Trick. Examination of the leading money-winning pacing colts and fillies from the recently concluded 2014 racing season provides ample testimony to just how totally influential Meadow Skipper really was.

Artspeak (Western Ideal-The Art Museum)

Last year's two-year old colt pacing champion is by Western Ideal, a son of Western Hanover from Leah Almahurst. Leah Almahurst is a granddaughter of Meadow Skipper, which sets up three distinct Meadow Skipper links on Artspeak's male side alone. The dam, Art Museum, provides three more links to Meadow Skipper through her sire Artsplace (from an Albatross mare), her dam Southwind Laurel by Matt's Scooter from a Meadow Skipper mare. In addition, Southwind Laurel's dam Luxury Class is by Jate Lobell, the first great son of No Nukes. This one can see six links back to Meadow Skipper in Artspeak's immediate pedigree.

JK She'salady (Art Major-Presidential Lady)

Last year's undefeated two-year-old pacing filly champion and horse of the year is by Art Major, who carries a double cross to Meadow Skipper through his sire Artsplace from an Albatross mare. Art Major's dam Perfect Profile is by Nihilator; he by the Albatross son Niatross. Nihilator's second dam Pretty Margie provides a third Meadow Skipper link. JK She'salady's dam, Presidential Lady, is by Presidential Ball, he by Most Happy Fella's son Cam Fella. Presidential Lady's dam is by Jamuga, a son of Meadow

Skipper, and her dam Pearl's Bunny, provides a link through her Albatross sire B.G.'s Bunny. In addition the second dam of Pearls Bunny, Jefferson Time, is a daughter of Meadow Skipper. Thus, one can see seven links to Meadow Skipper in the immediate pedigree of JK She'salady.

McWicked (McArdle-Western Sahara)

Last year's three-year-old pacing champion is by McArdle, he by Falcon Seelster from the Nihilator mare Lilting Laughter. Her dam Happy Sharon is a daughter of Most Happy Fella. This makes two direct links to Meadow Skipper. Nihilator's second dam, Pretty Margie, provides a third link, being a daughter of Meadow Skipper. McWicked's dam, Western Sahara, is by Western Hanover's son Western Ideal, which offers three more links to Meadow Skipper. McWicked's second dam, Banka Bella, is by the Albatross son Kiev Hanover from the Matt's Scooter mare Bunting, which adds three more links. Bunting's third dam, Buna Hanover, is by Albatross, adding the ninth link.

Color a Virgin (Always a Virgin-Full Color)

Last year's three-year-old pacing filly champion, the Indiana bred Color a Virgin is by Always a Virgin, he a son of Western Ideal, who, as documented above, provides three links to Meadow Skipper. Always a Virgin's second dam, Keystone Wallis, is from an Albatross mare that provides link number 4. Color a Virgin's dam, Full Color's sire, All American Ingot, a son of Western Hanover who himself provides two more links. All American Ingot's second dam, Queen Margie by Meadow Skipper, provides another link, number 7. Full Color's dam Broadway Approach is from Most Happy Fella's daughter, Above Board, which provides link number 8.

SWEET LOU (Yankee Cruiser-Sweet Future)

Last year's aged pacing champion is by Yankee Cruiser, who provides three links to Meadow Skipper through his sire Artiscape, he by Artsplace from an On the Road Again mare. Artsplace brings in the often-mentioned Albatross, while On the Road Again is by Most Happy Fellas' son Happy Motoring.

Yankee Cruiser's dam, A Yankee Classic, provides two more links through her Jate Lobell sire and dam Choice Yankee, she by the Albatross son Colt Fortysix. Sweet Lou's dam, Sweet Future, is by Falcon's Future, he from an Oil Burner dam that proves link number 6. Sweet Future's dam, Sweet Dahrlin, is by Meadow Skipper's son Nero, providing link number 7.

Anndrovette (Riverboat King-Easy Miss)

Last year's aged pacing mare champion is by Riverboat King, he by Cam's Card Shark from the No Nukes mare, Why Won't Ya. Cam's Card Shark, by Cam Fella from a B.G.'s Bunny mare, offers two Meadow Skipper links, while Why Won't Ya by No Nukes provides link number 3. Easy Miss is by Big Towner, who has not one Meadow Skipper link, being a foal of 1974 by the then thirty-year-old Gene Abbe. Her dam, Book Order by the Albatross son Three Wizards, provides link number 4.

Foiled Again (Dragon Again-In a Safe Place)

The all-time leading, money-winning pacing horse with earnings of $6,923,781 and climbing is by Dragon Again, he a Most Happy Fella great-grandson through his grandsire Tyler B. The dam of Dragon Again, Ever Again, links to Albatross through her third dam, Bertana Hanover.

Foiled Again's dam, In a Safe Place, is by Artsplace who has an Albatross dam. In a Safe Place is from the Dexter Nukes mare Sunshine Judy. Dexter Nukes by No Nukes, from Viking Princess by Albatross, provides two more links. Link number 6 stems from In a Safe Place's fourth dam Ata Connie, she by Meadow Skipper. Thus, the world's richest pacing horse, Foiled Again, has six Meadow Skipper links in his immediate pedigree.

Not that I'm tooting my own horn or anything like that, but where would this breed be if I were, heaven forbid, gelded as a two-year old?

Good question, Mr. Skipper, sir. That might be a question for the ages!

Meadow Skipper's final resting place

19

A Funeral Fit for a King

Somewhere, somewhere in time's own space,
Where creeks sing on and tall trees grow,
Some paradise where horses go.
For by the love that guides my pen,
I know great horses live again.

And now, the end is near
As I breed my final broodmare
My friends, I'll say it clear
At the start there were some crude mares
I paced the longest miles of any horse
on racetrack highway
And through each uncharted course
I did it my way!

—Meadow Skipper

RIP, Meadow Skipper

January 28, 1982
Stoner Creek Stud; Paris, Kentucky

It's an unusually mild April-like morning here at Stoner Creek Stud. The wind is gusting up a bit and the skies fluctuate between bluish and grayish. While physically I look and act like I always do, I have this sinking feeling that all is not right. Lately, I have been extremely tired, and my arthritis is noticeable. But then again, winter in Kentucky, other than today perhaps, is anything but balmy.

I've been reminiscing a lot lately, as I guess I'm supposed to at this stage of life. Been thinking about the wonderful life I've lived. I had a loving mother (Countess Vivian) and a great father (Dale Frost), who I never met, and he never really got the credit he deserved, although having me as his son opened some eyes as to the sire he really was. Hey, look,

I raced against two of Dale's other boys, Chapel Chief and Armbro Dale, and neither was a pushover. I even trained down the whole way as a five-year-old with my Dale Frost paternal brother, Steven Frost. really loved those endless trail ways down at Pinehurst.

I've been blessed with having some wonderful people in my life, starting with the Midas of Meadowlands Farm, Del Miller. Delvin had considerable patience putting up with my antics and laziness.

Mr. Norman Woolworth was the best owner any horse could ever have. He was an heir to the king of the five-and-dime store and was one hell of a guy! And could he ever come up with some super horse names too!

Then there's Earl Avery. Although the old man was tough on me, parking me out in almost all of my races, I suspect he somehow realized that I could handle those outside trips. With a finesse driver like Buddy Gilmour, I'd have won more races, but then no one, including me, would know how tough I really was.

As for the women in my life, there have been many, but only one that ever touched my old implacable heart! Her name was Laughing Girl, and she was this beautiful, dainty thing. Together we made glorious music, making our awesome son Most Happy Fella in addition to Jolly Roger and Good Humor Man. I kinda thought Good Humor Man might have been a tad too pretty and actually winced when I learned he sold for a whopping $210,000 at Tattersalls. Hey, Girl, we did some good, didn't we?

Sadly, Laughing Girl had an abbreviated life, dying at the age of nine after a pasture accident. When I heard about her passing, I was devastated, for I never got to say good-bye. I picked at my food and sulked a bit. (Yes, Mr. Delvin, I can still sulk.) I continued breeding mares because that's what stallions do. But no matter how hot or fast the other mares happened to be, Laughing Girl remained my special girl. I knew Laughing Girl would want me to go on and fulfill my destiny. Since Girl was also owned by Mr. Woolworth, she was buried in the cemetery at Stoner Creek, so I got to see her grave from time to time.

At about nine in the morning of January 28, as I was watching all the little ones in their morning frolic, I felt a sudden sharp pain in my chest. I remember collapsing and letting out a few whinnies. Next, I felt the stallion caretakers, Jewel Tucker and Jim Sheeler, vainly pounding on my chest, yelling for Bobby McDonald to call the veterinarian. I remember farm manager Tom Stewart desperately trying to administer oxygen. Dr. Thomas Swercek, who performed the autopsy at the university of Kentucky, said I had a heart attack that day. After twenty-two years of arduous use, my old ticker just stopped ticking.

Rumor has it when you die your whole life just flashes in front of you. Well, my friends, mine did. The first thing I saw was my mother, Countess Vivian, birthing me. What a traumatic experience that was! One minute I was nice and warm in there, and the next minute it was, "Egad, hello world!"

Although I was frightened, my mama licked my face to open my eyes and started comforting and cleaning me, and all was okay. Fast forward to the scene of this trainer person at Ben White Racetrack putting some kind of uncomfortable straps on my legs to aid in hitting the pace. I was hardly a happy camper wearing those things at first. You try strapping those things around your legs and then start pacing!

Next, I flashed to this winner's circle scene from the Cane at Yonkers, standing next to a beaming Mr. Woolworth and Earle Avery. This was the moment. It was the first time I beat the "superhorse," Overtrick. I'll never forget Overtrick. He was one fantastic bugger who beat me more than I beat him, but even when he won, he knew I was there. Although he might have been a more complete racehorse than I was, it was me who became the "superstud." Pay back's a bitch, eh, Overtrick?

When my racing career was over and I was turned out to be a stallion, I met the girl of my dreams. I was an eager young stud of six years old—you know, a little cocky—and then pow! In trotted this exquisitely dainty but smoking hot little virgin.

She had me with the first nicker. My heart went pitter-patter. I sensed she felt as I did, for our necks tenderly entwined. Yes, Mr. Tessio, you were so right on about the romance stuff between a stallion and a mare. Together we made our three sons. (But between you and me, Happy, as we called him, was my favorite!) Happy looked a lot like me, especially on the racetrack, and in the end he was as good as, if not an even better, dad than I was. You know, it's funny how you really do relive the good times and tend to discard those not-so-good times.

After they tried to resuscitate me to no avail, Mr. Woolworth made plans to have me embalmed before I was laid to rest! The expert mortician, Mr. Karl Lusk, Jr. of nearby Paris, Kentucky, performed the embalming procedure.

What an honor! I was the only Standardbred ever to be embalmed in the state of Kentucky. Then they lowered my solid oak wooden casket to the concrete vault dug into the cemetery ground, between the grave of the great thoroughbred Triple

Crown Champion Count Fleet and the headstone of trotting sire Rodney.

At precisely 2:15 on a raw and windy February 1 afternoon, they opened the casket and there I was, eyes closed, lying on my side with my knees bent. I didn't see a dry eye in that somber crowd.

About seventy-five members of prime bluegrass royalty were on hand that fateful Monday, including John Cashman, Albert Adams, Bill Waggoner, Steve Brown, and Schare Adams. The honorable Doug Castle, Mayor of Paris, Kentucky, was also present. Several people made speeches, and I remember Mr. Cashman mentioning how I so influenced the pacing breed and that my sons and daughters would continue to do so in the years to come. Mr. and Mrs. Stewart was standing there like proud but grieving parents—heads bowed and with tears dripping down their faces!

When the last person departed, I was suddenly engulfed in this strange, muted amber-colored light. I knew my embalmed body was lying in the casket, but then I saw what looked like an apparition of me floating upwards from the box and majestically rising through a luminous azure sky. I followed along, heading toward what looked like a fine mist-covered, reddish-brownish trailway trimmed in panoramic purple haze and surrounded by puffy clouds. I just trotted along like a carefree colt—no more pain, only freedom.

As I approached the highest peak in that trail, I became vaguely conscious of what seemed like such a familiar nicker. Suddenly I saw this huge flashing sign in pastel colors that read "The Rainbow Bridge."

There were dogs, cats, horses, and other animals playing and romping in what looked like endless meadows of emerald serenity. I remembered hearing one of my grooms mentioning this Rainbow Bridge the day her dog unexpectedly died. She was tearful, but she consoled herself, convinced they would meet again when it was her time to cross the Rainbow Bridge!

As I crossed over to the other side, once again I heard this familiar though definitely more prominent sound. Waiting for me at this primrose passage to paradise, looking ever-so-radiant and beautiful, was Laughing Girl. She was a vision, looking exactly the way she did that very first time I laid eyes on her. I trotted over and gently nuzzled that gorgeous face. Side by side, our tails held high. We were together again at last. Eternity awaits.

The Rainbow Bridge

Epilogue

It has been almost a half century since that warm morning at the Meadowlands Farm, the morning when the greatest sire since Adam was born. Just as fate and serendipity played a significant role in the birth and life of Meadow Skipper, so did these elements affect the origins of this book.

I have been involved in the harness business the past forty years in various aspects. My coauthor, Bob Marks, has been in it a little longer than I have. I had just finished writing the book *Roosevelt Raceway: Where It All Began* with my coauthors, Freddie Hudson and Billy Haughton Jr., when I ran into Bob at Sunshine Meadows. He was preparing for a sale that never got off the ground.

Anyone in the harness business knows that Bob Marks was the breeding and marketing expert at Perretti Farms and has bred, sold, and watched thousands of horses during his tenure. We are both advocates and love the business; it is our life. I never understood why standardbreds have always taken a backseat to the thoroughbreds, especially since the late eighties.

*What backseat? We work so much harder than thor-
oughbreds do and race far more often than those prima
donnas.*

Our industry is just as rewarding, if not more so, than the thoroughbreds, for our horses can be essential parts of our lives for many years.

Being frustrated and saddened that the harness industry no longer gets the recognition that it deserves, I asked Bob Marks, who will be inducted in the Hall of Fame this July, if he would cowrite a book with me. When he asked what the book would be about, I said, "Let's write about the Secretariat/Northern Dancer/Seabiscuit of harness racing."

He replied, "Then the book should be about Meadow Skipper, perhaps the greatest sire since Adam."

*I knew there was a reason why I chose you guys to write
my life story!*

Although there are many deserving trotters and pacers, perhaps the most unique is Meadow Skipper. Even today there is hardly a pacing horse that you cannot trace back to the great sire. He was a fairy tale horse. Almost an afterthought, as his mother had to be switched from being bred to Adios to the unsung and unproven Dale Frost. At age two, Meadow Skipper was slated to be gelded but managed to sufficiently redeem himself shoving those thoughts to the back burner.

In the beginning of his career as a stallion, he was provided very few of what could be termed "high-quality broodmares." Yet, defying almost insurmountable odds, he still conclusively changed the direction of the pacing breed. Back in Skipper's racing days, if you had a 2:00

pacer, that was excellent. Nowadays, Skipper's descendants are shattering teletimers with mind-boggling miles in the 1:47 range.

Some of us, like my coauthor, was lucky enough to have seen this phenomenal horse race live and in person; but most of us, unfortunately, were not that lucky. Bob and I are hoping that we have somehow brought this incredible equine back to life so that you can get to know and cherish him like we have come to.

I want to thank you two guys for patiently transcribing my story as it actually happened.

He was the *only* Standardbred in the history of harness racing to have been embalmed. Meadow Skipper was equine royalty, and there may never be another like him.

Well, my mother was a Countess, wasn't she?

Thanks, Skipper, for all you did for the industry, horsemen, and racing fans everywhere. There will be more horses that set faster records, but there can *never* be another you! We hope you, Laughing Girl (the love of your life), and son Most Happy Fella are pain-free and tranquil, roaming and grazing the great pasture in the sky.

About the Authors

Victoria M. Howard

Victoria Howard has been involved with Standardbred racehorses for forty years. She has trained, bred, and raced horses and once co-owned Efishnc who was the Two-Year-Old Pacing Filly of 1994. In recognition of her writings, relentless coaching, and empowering of women, Victoria was voted VIP Woman of the Year by Who's Who for Women Worldwide.

Ms. Howard has written and published ten books. Her first, *Why Women Love Bad Boys*, is now translated and sold in fifteen countries. In her earlier years, she held many beauty titles and once represented her state in the Mrs. USA Pageant.

Bob Marks

Bob Marks first went to Roosevelt Raceway in 1960 and got hooked on harness racing. He used to make the double header on Saturday's hitting Aqueduct in the afternoon then either Roosevelt or Yonkers at night.

Instead of a puppet, a poet, a pauper, a pirate, a pawn, or a king, Bob became a noted harness handicapper and writer published in all the trades. Later, as a breeder-consultant for leading breeding farms, he used his advertising background to create and write the ads and the audio scripts for stallion and yearling videos.

Meadow Skipper: The Untold Story represents his first attempt at being a coauthor.

Sources and References

The United States Trotting Association's *Pathway*

The Hall of Fame of The Trotter and the Harness Museum

Hoofbeats Magazine

The *Lexington Herald-Leader*

The *Horseman and Fair World* magazine

The *Harness Horse* magazine